A
Kids' Guide to the
Periodic Table

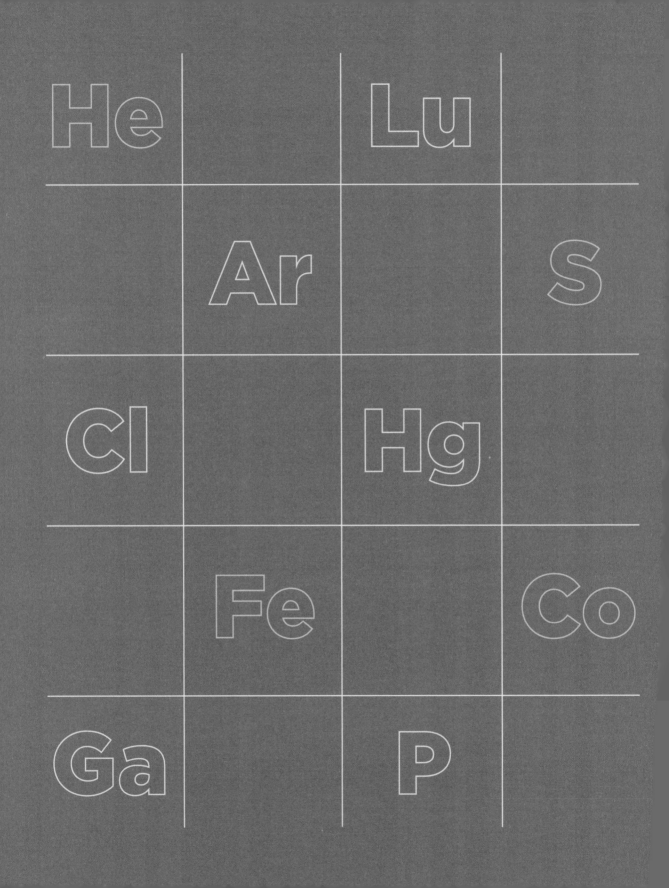

A Kids' Guide to the Periodic Table

Everything You Need to Know about the Elements

Edward P. Zovinka, PhD, and Rose A. Clark, PhD

callisto publishing
an imprint of Sourcebooks

Published by Callisto Publishing LLC C/O Sourcebooks LLC
P.O. Box 4410, Naperville, Illinois 60567-4410
(630) 961-3900
callistopublishing.com

This product conforms to all applicable CPSC and CPSIA standards.

Source of Production: 1010 Printing Asia Limited, Kwun Tong, Hong Kong, China
Date of Production: September 2023
Run Number: 5035334

Printed and Bound In China
OGP 20

We would like to dedicate this book to our beautiful children, who put up with all our science books, periodic tables, and, of course, chemistry experiments in our home.

Contents

1 HYDROGEN 22	2 HELIUM 23	3 LITHIUM 24	4 BERYLLIUM 25
11 SODIUM 32	12 MAGNESIUM 33	13 ALUMINUM 34	14 SILICON 35
21 SCANDIUM 42	22 TITANIUM 43	23 VANADIUM 44	24 CHROMIUM 45
31 GALLIUM 52	32 GERMANIUM 53	33 ARSENIC 54	34 SELENIUM 55
41 NIOBIUM 62	42 MOLYBDENUM 63	43 TECHNETIUM 64	44 RUTHENIUM 65
51 ANTIMONY 72	52 TELLURIUM 73	53 IODINE 74	54 XENON 75
61 PROMETHIUM 82	62 SAMARIUM 82	63 EUROPIUM 83	64 GADOLINIUM 84
71 LUTETIUM 90	72 HAFNIUM 91	73 TANTALUM 92	74 TUNGSTEN 93
81 THALLIUM 100	82 LEAD 101	83 BISMUTH 102	84 POLONIUM 103
91 PROTACTINIUM 110	92 URANIUM 111	93 NEPTUNIUM 112	94 PLUTONIUM 112
101 MENDELEVIUM 117	102 NOBELIUM 118	103 LAWRENCIUM 118	104 RUTHERFORDIUM 119
111 ROENTGENIUM 125	112 COPERNICIUM 126	113 NIHONIUM 127	114 FLEROVIUM 127

5 BORON 26	6 CARBON 27	7 NITROGEN 28	8 OXYGEN 29	9 FLUORINE 30	10 NEON 31
15 PHOSPHORUS 36	16 SULFUR 37	17 CHLORINE 38	18 ARGON 39	19 POTASSIUM 40	20 CALCIUM 41
25 MANGANESE 46	26 IRON 47	27 COBALT 48	28 NICKEL 49	29 COPPER 50	30 ZINC 51
35 BROMINE 56	36 KRYPTON 57	37 RUBIDIUM 58	38 STRONTIUM 59	39 YTTRIUM 60	40 ZIRCONIUM 61
45 RHODIUM 66	46 PALLADIUM 67	47 SILVER 68	48 CADMIUM 69	49 INDIUM 70	50 TIN 71
55 CESIUM 76	56 BARIUM 77	57 LANTHANUM 78	58 CERIUM 79	59 PRASEODYMIUM 80	60 NEODYMIUM 81
65 TERBIUM 85	66 DYSPROSIUM 86	67 HOLMIUM 87	68 ERBIUM 88	69 THULIUM 89	70 YTTERBIUM 89
75 RHENIUM 94	76 OSMIUM 95	77 IRIDIUM 96	78 PLATINUM 97	79 GOLD 98	80 MERCURY 99
85 ASTATINE 104	86 RADON 105	87 FRANCIUM 106	88 RADIUM 107	89 ACTINIUM 108	90 THORIUM 109
95 AMERICIUM 113	96 CURIUM 114	97 BERKELIUM 115	98 CALIFORNIUM 115	99 EINSTEINIUM 116	100 FERMIUM 117
105 DUBNIUM 120	106 SEABORGIUM 121	107 BOHRIUM 122	108 HASSIUM 123	109 MEITNERIUM 123	110 DARMSTADTIUM 124
115 MOSCOVIUM 128	116 LIVERMORIUM 128	117 TENNESSINE 129	118 OGANESSON 129		

Foreword

Hello, and welcome to the periodic table!

The periodic table is a complete listing of every element known to humans. It is the tool all scientists use to better understand the elements, the building blocks of everything in our world and beyond. The periodic table turned 150 years old in 2019, and the world spent the year celebrating this scientific marvel.

Who are we? Dr. Rose A. Clark is a professor of chemistry who specializes in analytical chemistry, using instruments to study the elements. Dr. Edward P. Zovinka is a professor of chemistry who focuses on the metals of the periodic table. We are both chemists at Saint Francis University in Pennsylvania and enjoy sharing our love of chemistry with students of all ages.

As chemists, we use and study the elements every day, so we are very familiar with the periodic table. We are excited to share the elements with you because they make up everything on the earth, in the solar system, and in the universe. You are uniquely you because of how the elements come together in your body. All of life on earth is the way it is because of the elements. And it's not just living things: The ink you see right now on the page is made up of carbon atoms, element #6 in the periodic table, which also makes up a lot of your body. The air you breathe is mostly nitrogen (element #7) and oxygen (#8). We hope that helps you understand the importance of the elements.

People have discovered 118 elements so far. Humans have known about and used elements like gold (#79) and iron (#26) for thousands of years, learning along the way about their unique properties. For example, gold is special because it does not react with other elements, so it stays shiny, while iron combines with carbon to make steel, which is strong enough to hold up buildings. Other elements, like oganesson (#118), are fairly new discoveries.

By learning about the elements, you can learn how our world works. So, join us on our journey to learn about the elements, how they are used, and how they were discovered. By doing so, you will be studying your past and your future!

EXPLORING ELEMENTS

The book you are reading is about the **periodic table** of the **elements**. Maybe you are wondering, what exactly is an element? That good question deserves a good answer.

Chemists have learned that elements are made up of **atoms**. Think of an atom as a sphere, like a golf ball—but a *lot* smaller. This sphere has three major parts: **protons**, **neutrons**, and **electrons**. The protons and neutrons are packed into the **nucleus**: the tiny, dense center of the atom. The protons have a positive charge, while neutrons have no charge. The electrons, which are negatively charged, fly around the nucleus. Every atom of an element has the same number of protons and electrons, keeping a balance of positives and negatives to make the atom neutral. The number of protons defines the element. If an element has 2 protons, it is helium (#2), the stuff that makes balloons float in the air. If an element has 13 protons, it is aluminum (#13), the material used to make soda cans.

While atoms are *really* small, almost all of their **mass** is packed in their even tinier nuclei. A typical atomic **radius** is 200 **picometers (pm)** or 2×10^{-10} meters. A typical nucleus is 20,000 times smaller: 10 femtometers or 1×10^{-14} meters. If we make the atom the size of a football stadium, the nucleus would be like a pencil eraser in the center of the stadium. The electrons would be somewhere in the stadium but would be smaller than your pencil tip (99.9999999999996% of atoms is empty space). Wow! Isn't that hard to imagine—and amazing?

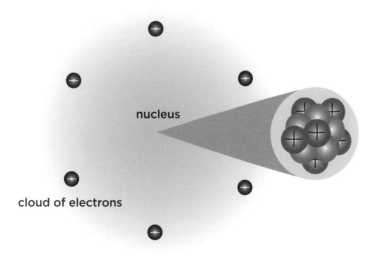

nucleus

cloud of electrons

When you start to look at the element profiles (page 22), you'll see that the illustration of each atom's nucleus shows only the protons and the neutrons. That's because electrons are so small, and there's so much empty space in an atom, that the electrons wouldn't even be on the page if the protons and neutrons were as big as we're showing them!

Elements are all around us now, but they are made in stars. As stars provide heat and light to our world, they also make new elements. Smaller atoms, like hydrogen (#1), smash into other small elements, like lithium (#3), to form something new. Let's do the math: What does 3 + 1 equal? For a chemist, 3 protons + 1 proton = 4 protons. That makes the element beryllium (#4). That type of math and chemistry is constantly occurring in many stars across the universe, creating additional quantities of our elements all the time.

DISCOVERY ZONE

Hennig Brand, a physician, was the first person credited for discovering an element, back in 1669. When he discovered phosphorus (#15), people already knew about elements like copper (#29), zinc (#30), silver (#47), and gold (#79). Other elements were discovered in the 1700s, bringing our collection up to 40 elements. However, it was Sir Humphry Davy who made elemental discovery a scientific process. From 1807 to 1808, Davy discovered seven new elements using the exciting new tool of **electrochemistry**! He passed an electric current through heated minerals to separate and collect the elements potassium (#19), sodium (#11), calcium (#20), strontium (#38), barium (#56), magnesium (#12), and boron (#5). Davy's electrochemistry method was the main tool used to discover more elements until 50 years later, when Robert Bunsen and Gustav Kirchhoff used the new **spectroscope** to discover elements by the light they absorb—a method still used today.

CHEMISTRY THROUGH THE AGES

Alchemists are often pictured in television shows and movies as old people wearing funny hats trying to make gold from lead. In reality, alchemists also viewed gold as a symbol of perfection, and they studied the universe to help make humankind better.

Out of their studies came chemistry and a number of other areas of science, such as psychology and medicine. Historians have found alchemists in cultures all around the world. Chinese alchemists made potions to help people reach harmony with the world. By studying the world around them, Greek alchemists gave us the idea that the world was made up of four elements—fire, air, earth, and water—all made from small unbreakable parts, which they called "*atomos*," or indivisible. That idea caused a lot of arguments over the centuries. Aristotle, the ancient Greek philosopher, rejected the idea because he saw no evidence of atoms. It

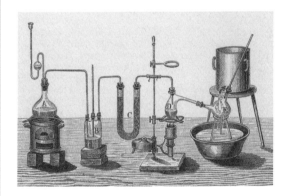

was not until John Dalton wrote the atomic theory in 1803 that alchemy changed into chemistry.

What took so long? You may have noticed that not all new ideas are accepted as good ones. People often like to stick to what they know. And people knew alchemists weren't always the most honest people. Some even tried to trick people with promises of making gold. Then along came Dalton, a meteorologist, who used the developing study of gases to explain the behavior of air based on atoms. He calculated atomic masses from the makeup of **compounds**. His work led scientists to accept the concept of indivisible atoms and helped make chemistry the math-focused science we know and use today.

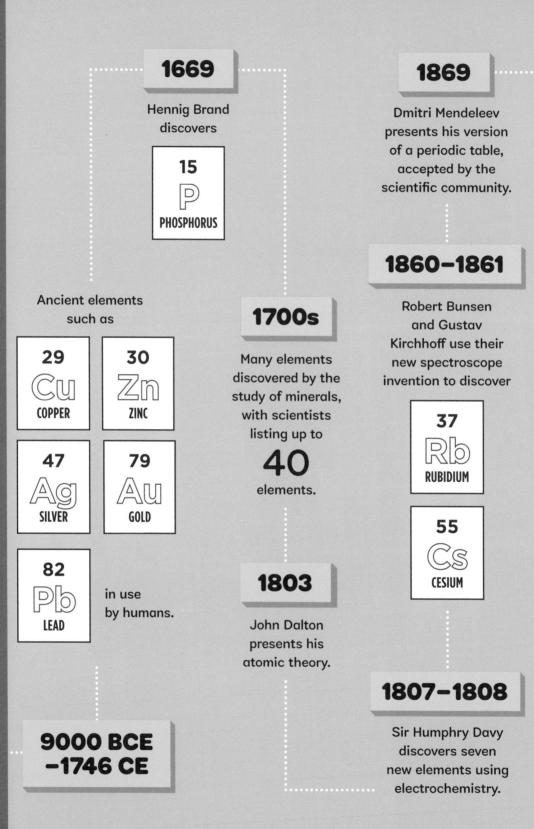

1669

Hennig Brand
discovers

15
P
PHOSPHORUS

1869

Dmitri Mendeleev
presents his version
of a periodic table,
accepted by the
scientific community.

1860–1861

Robert Bunsen
and Gustav
Kirchhoff use their
new spectroscope
invention to discover

37
Rb
RUBIDIUM

55
Cs
CESIUM

Ancient elements
such as

29	30
Cu	Zn
COPPER	ZINC

47	79
Ag	Au
SILVER	GOLD

82
Pb
LEAD

in use
by humans.

1700s

Many elements
discovered by the
study of minerals,
with scientists
listing up to

40

elements.

1803

John Dalton
presents his
atomic theory.

1807–1808

Sir Humphry Davy
discovers seven
new elements using
electrochemistry.

**9000 BCE
–1746 CE**

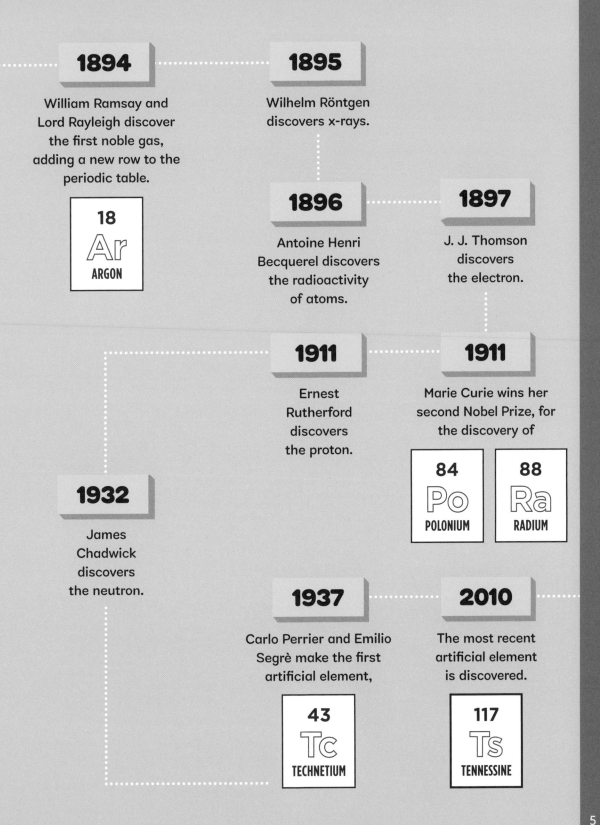

1894

William Ramsay and Lord Rayleigh discover the first noble gas, adding a new row to the periodic table.

| 18 |
| Ar |
| ARGON |

1895

Wilhelm Röntgen discovers x-rays.

1896

Antoine Henri Becquerel discovers the radioactivity of atoms.

1897

J. J. Thomson discovers the electron.

1911

Ernest Rutherford discovers the proton.

1911

Marie Curie wins her second Nobel Prize, for the discovery of

84	88
Po	Ra
POLONIUM	RADIUM

1932

James Chadwick discovers the neutron.

1937

Carlo Perrier and Emilio Segrè make the first artificial element,

| 43 |
| Tc |
| TECHNETIUM |

2010

The most recent artificial element is discovered.

| 117 |
| Ts |
| TENNESSINE |

TAKING APART THE ATOM

Because of a great amount of research by scientists such as Rutherford, Chadwick, and Thomson, we know the atom has three main parts—the proton, neutron, and electron. The proton and neutron reside in the nucleus, the tiny part at the center of the atom containing most of the atom's mass. The protons are positively charged, while the neutrons have no charge (neutral). Neutrons' lack of charge plays an important role in making all the elements on the periodic table. An important fact in physics is that positive charges repel each other. So, if there were too many protons in the nucleus, the nucleus would fly apart. By placing a neutron between protons, we keep the like-charged protons away from each other. Let's look at gold (#79). Because it is element #79, it has 79 protons. To keep 79 protons from flying away from each other, we need to surround the protons with a lot of neutral packing material—118 neutrons. The total mass would be 79 + 118 = 197.

Electrons, which are negatively charged, are super important to chemists. The sharing (or not sharing) of electrons decides how the element will react. Chemists think of the electrons as whizzing around the nucleus of an atom. But electrons are complex materials. They don't follow easily defined pathways like the moon's orbit around the earth. Even stranger, electrons act as *both* a particle and a wave, depending on how you test them. A **particle** is a small object that takes up a defined spot in space, like a ball sitting on the ground. A **wave** is a disturbance that travels through space, with peaks and dips, like light and sound. If you set up a test to determine the mass of electrons (how much they

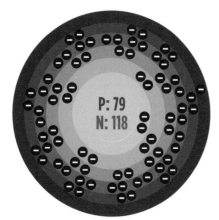

weigh), you can measure the mass of the particle. But if you set up a test to treat them like a wave in motion, they behave like a wave. In chemistry, sometimes the weirdness is part of the fun!

Atomic properties are the ways in which we characterize an element. The properties important to a chemist include the atomic number, atomic mass, **density**, and atomic radius.

ATOMIC PROPERTIES

Atomic Number

The atomic number is the key to understanding the periodic table. The atomic number refers to the number of protons in the nucleus of the atom and makes each element unique. For example, take a look at the simplest element, hydrogen (#1). It has one proton. It has an atomic number of 1. Anything with one proton, and only one proton, will be a hydrogen atom. We build the periodic table using the atomic numbers. Helium (#2) has 2 protons. In this book, the atomic number will be shown above the element symbol.

Atomic Mass

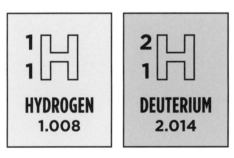

The atomic mass is the sum of the number of protons and the number of neutrons in an atom, measured in **atomic mass units**, or amu. Electrons are so small that they do not change the total mass. Remember, the number of protons is always the same for an element. But the atomic mass can be different from one atom to another. Let's take a look at an example using hydrogen. Hydrogen can exist with just one proton. Yet it can be found (or made) in three different forms—one with no neutron, a version with one neutron (deuterium), and a third version with two neutrons. Notice they all have one proton so they are *all* hydrogen, but the three forms have different atomic masses. These are **isotopes** of hydrogen.

Density

Density is a useful tool in identifying elements, as each one has a unique density. Density is defined as the mass of an object divided by the volume the mass occupies. Mass refers to the amount of physical matter that makes up an object. Take a cheese cube, 2 centimeters (or cm) by 2 cm by 2 cm. Determine the volume of your cube. The volume will be length times width times height; using the data above, it will be 8 cm³. You can get the mass of the cheese by putting it on a scientific balance (the cube weighs 8.71 grams, abbreviated as g). Finally, take your mass and divide it by the volume. In this case, we take 8.71 g and divide it by 8 cm³, giving us the math answer of 1.09 g/cm³. The g/cm³ unit is commonly used by chemists. You will also see density listed as g/mL, but 1 mL equals 1 cm³! What is the density of the cheese? It is 1.09 g/mL. Try this again with a block of cheese in your refrigerator; the mass in grams is on the label. Measure the dimensions in centimeters. The density for the whole block will be the same as for a piece that's just 2 cm³.

Atomic Radius

Chemists like to use atomic radius to compare the sizes of the elements and to help us explain chemical observations. Measuring the atomic radius is just like measuring the radius of a ball: It is the distance from the center of the ball to its outer edge. You can't see atoms because they are very small. A hydrogen atom is 31 picometers (pm); 31 picometers is 0.000000000031 of a meter (a very small fraction of a meter). Look up the radius of hydrogen yourself. Did you find different numbers, like 50 pm? Since the atomic radius depends on the number of electrons in the element and the type of measurement you use, you can get different numbers for the radius (see "Taking Apart the Atom," page 6). As a general trend, atoms get bigger as you go down the periodic table. As you go across a row on the periodic table, the atomic radius gets smaller.

THE PERIODIC TABLE

Almost everyone has seen a periodic table hanging on the wall in school or in a museum. Many people learn about the periodic table in a science class, and definitely in a high school chemistry class. Most of us see the standard periodic table introduced to the world by Russian chemist Dmitri Mendeleev. There are a number of columns and rows, and each of the 118 elements is shown by its own one- or two-letter symbol.

The standard periodic table is arranged in order of increasing atomic numbers, so you see H, hydrogen, as the first element with 1 proton. Next, you see He, helium, with two protons, and so on. Eventually, we reach the end of a row of elements and start a new row below. Besides the rows, there are columns of elements. The columns and rows are both important to chemists for different reasons. We will focus on the elements in the same column because they have similar chemical properties.

For example, that whole first column of the periodic table, which includes lithium and sodium, is called the alkali metal family of elements. The elements in the second column are called the alkaline earth metals. Some chunks of the table are grouped together and go across rows instead of down columns. We will learn about the families first and then jump into the elements in a little more detail and explain some exciting uses of each.

DISCOVERY ZONE

Dmitri Mendeleev is the chemist most commonly given credit for preparing the periodic table. Mendeleev built his table using information available from the hard work of many chemists before him. The idea of the periodic table came to be important to Mendeleev when he was writing a chemistry book and needed a way to readily explain the elements to the readers. He ordered the elements by atomic mass because the proton had not yet been discovered.

THE PERIODIC TABLE

	1	2	3	4	5	6	7	8	9
HYDROGEN									
1	**1** H HYDROGEN	**ALKALI METALS**							
2	**3** Li LITHIUM	**4** Be BERYLLIUM	**ALKALINE EARTH METALS**						
3	**11** Na SODIUM	**12** Mg MAGNESIUM						**TRANSITION METALS**	
4	**19** K POTASSIUM	**20** Ca CALCIUM	**21** Sc SCANDIUM	**22** Ti TITANIUM	**23** V VANADIUM	**24** Cr CHROMIUM	**25** Mn MANGANESE	**26** Fe IRON	**27** Co COBALT
5	**37** Rb RUBIDIUM	**38** Sr STRONTIUM	**39** Y YTTRIUM	**40** Zr ZIRCONIUM	**41** Nb NIOBIUM	**42** Mo MOLYBDENUM	**43** Tc TECHNETIUM	**44** Ru RUTHENIUM	**45** Rh RHODIUM
6	**55** Cs CESIUM	**56** Ba BARIUM	57-71	**72** Hf HAFNIUM	**73** Ta TANTALUM	**74** W TUNGSTEN	**75** Re RHENIUM	**76** Os OSMIUM	**77** Ir IRIDIUM
7	**87** Fr FRANCIUM	**88** Ra RADIUM	89-103	**104** Rf RUTHERFORDIUM	**105** Db DUBNIUM	**106** Sg SEABORGIUM	**107** Bh BOHRIUM	**108** Hs HASSIUM	**109** Mt MEITNERIUM

	57	58	59	60	61	62	63
LANTHANIDES	**57** La LANTHANUM	**58** Ce CERIUM	**59** Pr PRASEODYMIUM	**60** Nd NEODYMIUM	**61** Pm PROMETHIUM	**62** Sm SAMARIUM	**63** Eu EUROPIUM
ACTINIDES	**89** Ac ACTINIUM	**90** Th THORIUM	**91** Pa PROTACTINIUM	**92** U URANIUM	**93** Np NEPTUNIUM	**94** Pu PLUTONIUM	**95** Am AMERICIUM

OF ELEMENTS

	10	11	12	13	14	15	16	17	18

	BORON FAMILY	CARBON FAMILY	PNICTOGENS	CHALCOGENS	HALOGENS	

2 He HELIUM — 1

5 B BORON	6 C CARBON	7 N NITROGEN	8 O OXYGEN	9 F FLUORINE	10 Ne NEON	2
13 Al ALUMINUM	14 Si SILICON	15 P PHOSPHORUS	16 S SULFUR	17 Cl CHLORINE	18 Ar ARGON	3

28 Ni NICKEL	29 Cu COPPER	30 Zn ZINC	31 Ga GALLIUM	32 Ge GERMANIUM	33 As ARSENIC	34 Se SELENIUM	35 Br BROMINE	36 Kr KRYPTON	4
46 Pd PALLADIUM	47 Ag SILVER	48 Cd CADMIUM	49 In INDIUM	50 Sn TIN	51 Sb ANTIMONY	52 Te TELLURIUM	53 I IODINE	54 Xe XENON	5
78 Pt PLATINUM	79 Au GOLD	80 Hg MERCURY	81 Tl THALLIUM	82 Pb LEAD	83 Bi BISMUTH	84 Po POLONIUM	85 At ASTATINE	86 Rn RADON	6
110 Ds DARMSTADTIUM	111 Rg ROENTGENIUM	112 Cn COPERNICIUM	113 Nh NIHONIUM	114 Fl FLEROVIUM	115 Mc MOSCOVIUM	116 Lv LIVERMORIUM	117 Ts TENNESSINE	118 Og OGANESSON	7

64 Gd GADOLINIUM	65 Tb TERBIUM	66 Dy DYSPROSIUM	67 Ho HOLMIUM	68 Er ERBIUM	69 Tm THULIUM	70 Yb YTTERBIUM	71 Lu LUTETIUM
96 Cm CURIUM	97 Bk BERKELIUM	98 Cf CALIFORNIUM	99 Es EINSTEINIUM	100 Fm FERMIUM	101 Md MENDELEVIUM	102 No NOBELIUM	103 Lr LAWRENCIUM

THE ELEMENT GROUPS

The elements are organized in the periodic table based on their atomic numbers and chemical properties. The elements' structures define how they will interact with each other and therefore define reactivity. For example, sodium (#11) and potassium (#19) are both in the first column. When either is placed in water, a fast and fizzy reaction occurs. They both seem to disappear in the water from their shiny elemental form. The change is a good indication of a chemical reaction.

Chemists also discovered that lithium (#3), rubidium (#37), cesium (#55), and francium (#87) all had the same sort of reactions when placed in water. So, chemists placed them in the same column. But why do they react this way? It all has to do with electrons.

The movement of electrons controls the chemistry of elements. Remember, your atom has the protons and neutrons in the nucleus, and the electrons are outside the nucleus, so electrons are easiest to lose or add. The first-column elements want to give away (lose) one electron to other elements or compounds. The elements of the second column want to give away two electrons.

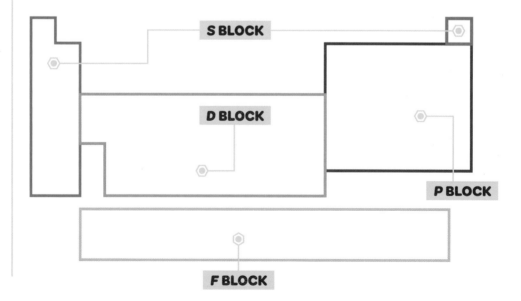

S BLOCK

D BLOCK

P BLOCK

F BLOCK

After the second column is the transition metal region, made up of 10 columns. Transition metal chemistry is interesting because these elements use a different set of electrons. Electrons get sorted into different places, called orbitals. Orbitals are like different drawers for stowing electrons. The elements in the first two columns use electrons from one "drawer," while the transition elements pick their electrons from a bigger "drawer," changing the chemical reactions that are possible. Electrons can be put into four main "drawers," giving us the four main parts of the periodic table. The four main regions are named the *s* block, the *p* block, the *d* block (transition metals), and the *f* block (lanthanides/actinides).

The majority of the elements on the periodic table are **metals** and want to give up an electron. A small section of the *p* block elements are **nonmetals** and want to gain an electron. A good chemical rule of thumb to remember is the octet rule, which states that elements like to **bond** so that each atom has eight electrons in its outer layer of electrons. If a metal and a nonmetal react, a compound is formed. If two nonmetals react, they share electrons and a **molecule** is formed. So, chemists see similarities down a column (a family) but also within certain rows, like the transition metals. With so many elements and possible combinations, scientists get to experiment and make millions of different compounds and molecules.

FAMILIES OF THE PERIODIC TABLE

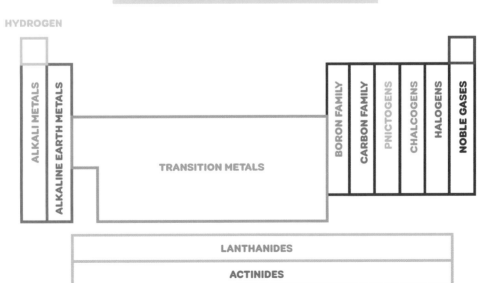

Hydrogen

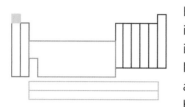

Hydrogen is a special and unique element. It is the first element on the periodic table. It is the fuel of stars like our sun, which makes life on the earth possible. Without the heat and light created by the sun, we would not be able to live on Earth. But hydrogen is even more special because of the process of creating the light and heat, which is called **fusion**. The sun combines two hydrogens to make a new atom, helium.

And you can combine one helium with one hydrogen to make a new atom, lithium. In other words, the stars are the element makers for the universe, all from hydrogen. Not too bad for the simplest element, made up of only 1 proton and 1 electron.

Chemists like to argue about what group hydrogen belongs in, often treating it as its own special, one-element group. While it falls into group 1, it is also seen in Column 17 (the halogens).

Alkali Metals

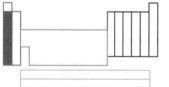

The alkali metals are the first column of the periodic table, often called group 1. Alkali is a word meaning that a chemical is a base (producing a pH greater than 7).

When placed in water, each of the elements in the column completes a very fast reaction, converting the element metal into a **salt** that is a base.

$$2\ Cs + 2H_2O \rightarrow 2CsOH\ (base) + H_2$$

As you look down the table, from lithium to francium, the reaction gets faster and faster.

And while most modern chemists use the word "base" instead of alkali, the name has stuck.

Alkaline Earth Metals

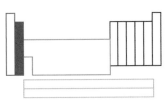

The alkaline earth metals are the second column. And like the alkali metals, these all react with water to form a base.

$$Ca + 2\ H_2O \rightarrow Ca(OH)_2 + H_2\ (g)$$

The name comes from early chemists trying to understand the elements and their reactions. Before knowing these elements, Antoine Lavoisier labeled compounds like $Ca(OH)_2$ as "alkaline earths" because they would not dissolve in water easily (more like dirt or earth) and they were hard to study.

Transition Metals

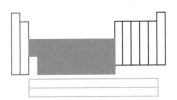

Transition metals include elements you use or see every day. Grouped with the transition metals are silver, gold, iron, and copper. We use these metals in our homes, our bodies, and our electronic devices.

They are a large group, running from columns 3 through 12. The electrons they share can be from more than one drawer (s-, p-, and d-block), making their chemistry a little more complicated but oh so much more fun for chemists.

Transition metals can help speed up a reaction and can commonly bond to six or seven other elements, making them the bonding envy of the other elements!

Boron Family

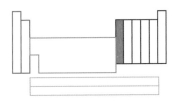

The boron family, while named after the non-metal boron, is actually dominated by a bunch of metals.

Aluminum, gallium, indium, and thallium—the other members of the family—are all metals. They are all in the same family because they all have filled the s drawer (chemists call it the s block) of electrons and are now starting a new drawer of electrons, the p drawer (p block).

They have found common use in **semiconductors**, so when you use a phone or computer, you will be using many of the group 13 elements.

Carbon Family

In group 14, carbon grabs all the attention of the carbon family. There are more molecules using the element carbon than any other element in the family and the whole periodic table!

The study of carbon is so important that chemists devote a whole field of study to carbon molecules and reactions. It's called organic chemistry.

Because all of these elements have two electrons in their *s* drawer and two electrons in the *p* drawer, they often make four bonds to other elements, although lead, way at the bottom of the family, is a bit of an exception.

Pnictogens

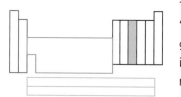

The "p" in "pnictogens" is silent, similar to the "p" in "pneumonia." So you pronounce the group name as "nictogen," even though there is a funny *p* out front. The name refers to the nonbreathability of pure nitrogen.

Remember, air is 21% oxygen and 78% nitrogen. If you get much below 21% oxygen, you may feel woozy or even sick, and you cannot live without oxygen.

The pnictogens are a mix of nonmetals (like nitrogen, phosphorus, and arsenic) and metals (such as antimony and bismuth). Pretty much all these elements are harmful on their own, so a chemist must be careful while studying group 15.

Chalcogens

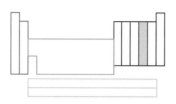

Chalcogens make up column 16 of the periodic table. In addition to oxygen, this group of elements includes sulfur, selenium, tellurium, polonium, and livermorium.

The term *chalcogen* is an old mining reference meaning "forming of ores." An ore is a material miners dig up in order to get the valuable metal out of it.

Many of the metal compounds miners dig up are compounds with oxygen and sulfur, as well as the other elements of the chalcogen family such as selenium and tellurium.

You may have heard of "fool's gold," a beautiful, shiny material that is an ore made of iron and sulfur, not gold! Notice, we didn't talk about polonium because it is **radioactive** and does not stay around long enough to make many valuable ores.

Halogens

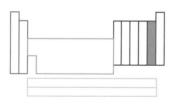

The halogens are the second to last column of the periodic table, group 17. There are six nonmetals in this family: fluorine, chlorine, bromine, iodine, astatine, and tennessine.

They are the most reactive elements on the table, except for maybe the alkali metals. They react very fast, trying to grab the one electron needed to complete their electron shell and have the same number of electrons as the unreactive (and noble!) gases.

Halogens like chlorine want to add one electron, and alkali metals like sodium want to lose one electron, so they can easily react with each other to form a salt, such as sodium chloride.

Noble Gases

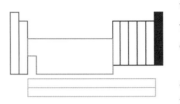

We sometimes think of the noble gases as the hidden gases. They simply don't do much chemistry!

When we teach chemistry, the noble gases are important because at the end of a row, the outer layer is filled with as many electrons as it can hold. Because the shell is full, these elements do not share or give up electrons too easily.

This stability makes them very special, and it also made them very hard to find. In fact, the noble gases were not discovered until about 25 years after Mendeleev's periodic table was published.

Lord Rayleigh and William Ramsay's discovery of the noble gases required a whole new column to be tacked on to the end of the table. Their research spurred more research about just where the electrons are in an atom, leading to a new division in science: quantum mechanics!

Lanthanides

The lanthanide group is actually a row, not a column. And they are kind of out of place on the periodic table. If you look carefully at the periodic table, notice that barium (#56) and hafnium (#72) are right next to each other. How odd. What happened to the missing 14 elements?

They are the lanthanides, usually placed as a separate row below the rest of the table. They are also referred to as the **rare earth elements**, even though they are not that hard to find!

Most of these elements use a new drawer of electrons: the *f* drawer (again, chemists call it the *f* block). All these elements have become very important in our tech-driven world and will play an important role in your life.

Actinides

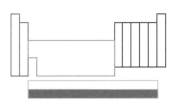

The actinides, like the lanthanides, are somewhat out of place. They follow radium (#88), are placed in their own separate row, and are all radioactive.

A radioactive element is one whose nucleus can break apart into smaller pieces, releasing energy and creating at least one other element on the periodic table. Remember, if the number of protons changes, you have a different element.

Radioactive elements can be dangerous and must be handled carefully. Radioactive elements handled properly also have many wonderful uses, from generating energy to making smoke detectors.

ELEMENTS IN THE HUMAN BODY

There are 118 elements on the periodic table but only 6 are major components of the human body: Oxygen, carbon, hydrogen, nitrogen, calcium (1.5%), and phosphorus (1%). Iron, potassium, sulfur, sodium, chlorine, zinc, copper, iodine, and magnesium make up the other elements your body needs for life. Just because the percentages of potassium (0.4%) and sodium (0.2%) are low does not mean they are not important. Your cells in your brain would not work without these two elements. You also could not live without iron (0.006%), as it is vital to bringing the oxygen from your lungs to all of the cells of your body! Other metals are found in the human body but are in very low concentrations (trace metals).

COMPOUNDS, MOLECULES, AND REACTIONS

We just talked about all the families in the periodic table and how each family has its own special reactivity. The alkali metals react by losing one electron and the halogens (nonmetals) react by gaining one electron. If we combine one alkali and one halogen, we form a compound called a salt. So if potassium reacts with fluorine (#9), an **ionic bond** forms the salt (the K^+ ion interacts with the F^- ion to make KF) potassium fluoride. If two nonmetals like hydrogen and oxygen react, they form a **covalent bond**, where they share electrons to make the molecule we call water (H_2O). If carbon and oxygen (nonmetals) react, another very important molecule is formed—carbon dioxide (CO_2). Trees and plants need carbon dioxide to make sugar so they can grow.

When we burn carbon in the form of natural gas to heat our homes, the carbon interacts with the oxygen in the air to produce carbon dioxide and water, as shown below.

$$CH_4 + 2\ O_2 \rightarrow CO_2 + 2\ H_2O$$

Reactants are shown on the left of the arrow, and the products of the reaction are shown on the right of the arrow. This equation represents a methane **combustion** (burning) reaction, in which methane is reacting with oxygen to create carbon dioxide and water. This is a balanced equation because you have the same number of carbon, hydrogen, and oxygen atoms on both sides of the arrow. This reaction is exothermic, meaning that energy is released as a result.

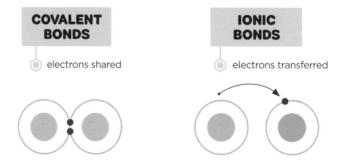

COVALENT BONDS	IONIC BONDS
electrons shared	electrons transferred

The 118 Elements

HYDROGEN

ELEMENTAL STATS

P+ 1
E- 1
N 0

State: Gas
Atomic Mass:
1.01 amu
Density:
0.082 g/L
Atomic Radius:
110 pm
Element Group:
Hydrogen

Hydrogen is the first element on our journey exploring the periodic table. It is the most abundant element in our universe and the 10th most abundant element in the earth's crust. While it is the simplest element, with just one proton and one electron, hydrogen is so important to us. It is a part of almost every molecule on Earth. Hydrogen makes up part of water (H_2O), it is an important part of gasoline (C_8H_{18}), and a lot of it is in our DNA (the instruction manual in every cell in our bodies).

In the **gas phase**, H_2 has a very low density—0.082 g/L. Compare that to the density of water, 1,000 g/L; that's so low that it's not held down by the planet's gravity and it escapes into our atmosphere. You may know this because hydrogen, like helium balloons, will float away in air.

Hydrogen exists as two atoms bonded together and is very flammable, so keep it away from matches. Its flammability also makes it quite useful. The National Aeronautics and Space Administration (NASA) has used hydrogen as fuel, combining liquid hydrogen with liquid oxygen (#8) to make a powerful explosion to push rockets into space.

Hydrogen is the heart and fuel of many stars. Stars generate their heat and light as they combine hydrogen atoms to make new elements. In fact, our next element, helium (#2), is made in the stars when the nuclei of hydrogen atoms combine through **nuclear fusion**. During fusion, atoms do not just share electrons like in a bond but combine their protons into one new nucleus.

Discovery Zone Robert Boyle discovered hydrogen in 1671, but he did not realize it was an element at the time. He was too busy studying gas behavior (Boyle's Law) to understand that it was a distinct element. Henry Cavendish was the first to realize that Boyle's discovery was, in fact, the element hydrogen.

HYDROGEN

HELIUM

We are sure you have used helium before. Have you ever gone to a birthday party and brought home a balloon that floats in the air? The balloon was filled with helium. Helium is in the noble gas family and is a very light gas, with a mass of just 4 amu. The majority of the air around us is nitrogen (#7) gas, which is much heavier (28 amu, N_2), so helium rises.

Many scientists use liquid helium to keep their instruments cold. Liquid helium has a temperature of –268.93°C, or –452.07°F, and will not stay around very long. Helium is the second most abundant element in the universe, but it makes up only 0.0005% of Earth's atmosphere. Because helium is so light, it also escapes our atmosphere and goes into space.

It is very rare to find helium on Earth, so we may experience a shortage of helium. You may have noticed this if you have ever visited party stores to get helium for balloons only to be told that they were out.

Discovery Zone
On a scientific expedition to India in 1868, Pierre Janssen measured the solar spectrum during a total eclipse. Each element absorbs light in a unique way, creating lines. Janssen observed a yellow line not previously reported by scientists. This provided evidence that the sun contains more than hydrogen (#1). At first, Janssen thought the new line was from sodium (#11), but then Joseph Norman Lockyer also observed the new yellow line while studying the sun. Because the element was discovered by observing the sun, it was named helium from the Greek *helios*, meaning "sun."

ELEMENTAL STATS

P+ 2
E- 2
N 2

State: Gas

Atomic Mass:
4 amu

Density:
0.00164 g/mL

Atomic Radius:
140 pm

Element Group:
Noble Gases

HELIUM

LITHIUM

ELEMENTAL STATS

P+ 3
E- 3
N commonly 4

State: Solid

Atomic Mass:
6.94 amu

Density:
0.534 g/cm³

Atomic Radius:
182 pm

Element Group:
Alkali Metals

Lithium is the first alkali metal. Lithium is added to ceramics to improve their strength and keep them from changing size at high temperatures, but batteries are the main use for lithium today. In fact, more than half of all the mined lithium is used in batteries, and most cell phones have lithium batteries.

Lithium batteries have become way more important over the last 10 years because of the newly developed rechargeable lithium ion battery (Li⁺). This type of battery is popular because a small one can provide a lot of energy. Most of us like our phones, games, and other electronics to be easily transported yet hold a charge for a long time.

Lithium for batteries is usually dug up from mines in Australia or Chile. You may think that you or your parents carry your phone around a lot, but think about the traveling your battery has done just to get to you!

Discovery Zone Lithium was discovered in 1817 by Swedish scientist Johan Arfwedson in the the mineral petalite. As was often the case with early element discoveries, Arfwedson did not collect the pure element. In the early 1800s, scientists were just developing the tools and tricks needed to purify the elements. A tiny amount of pure lithium was collected in 1821, but it wasn't isolated in large quantities until 1855.

LITHIUM

BERYLLIUM

4

Be

Beryllium is found in the earth's crust, mostly in volcanic rocks. It is also found in beautiful gemstones, like emerald and aquamarine. The state of Utah supplies nearly two-thirds of the beryllium metal used in the world.

Beryllium is one of our two lightest metals (lithium [#3] being the lightest) and is a silvery white metal in the alkaline earth family on the periodic table. It does not react with air or water, as a lot of the alkaline earth metals do. When it is mixed with other metals, like copper (#29) and nickel (#28), beryllium helps improve their chemical properties. The mixed metals (**alloys**) become better at conducting electricity and heat. Beryllium also makes alloys springier, so think about that next time you jump or bounce on a mattress.

As a pure metal, beryllium is dangerous, causing miners to get sick if it gets in their lungs. Beryllium was used to help discover the neutron, an important part of the atom. In 1932, James Chadwick smashed alpha rays (which are helium nuclei) into a sample of beryllium. He observed that beryllium emitted a new kind of subatomic particle, which had mass but no charge—the neutron!

 Discovery Zone The gemstones beryl and emerald are both forms of beryllium aluminum silicate, $Be_3Al_2(SiO_3)_6$. Mineralogist Abbé René-Just Haüy thought beryl and emerald might contain a new element, so he asked chemist Nicolas-Louis Vauquelin to experiment with them. In 1798, Vauquelin announced his discovery of the element and named the element glaucinium (Greek *glykys* = sweet) because its compounds tasted sweet. (Never taste your chemistry experiments!) Others preferred the name *beryllium*, based on the gemstone, and this is now its official name.

ELEMENTAL STATS

P+ 4
E- 4
N 5

State: Solid

Atomic Mass: 9.01 amu

Density: 1.85 g/cm³

Atomic Radius: 153 pm

Element Group: Alkaline Earth Metals

BERYLLIUM

ELEMENTAL STATS

P+ 5
E- 5
N 5 or 6

State: Solid

Atomic Mass:
10.81 amu

Density:
2.37 g/cm³

Atomic Radius:
192 pm

Element Group:
Boron Family

BORON

Have you ever made slime from mixing borax solution with glue? If so, then you have used a boron compound! Borax, $Na_2B_4O_7 \cdot 10H_2O$, is not only a great soap, but it is also a great slime maker!

Boron is also essential for the cell walls of plants. It is not considered poisonous to animals, but in higher doses, it can upset the body's metabolism. So, always wash your hands after making slime. It is not all bad, though. We take in about 2 mg of boron each day from our food, which helps keep our bones healthy.

The most important boron compounds include boric acid, borax (sodium borate), and boric oxide. These can be found in eye drops, antiseptics, washing powders, and tile glazes. More exciting is the use of boron in fireworks, giving us a cool, green color for celebrations! Chemists depend on boron almost every day. Borosilicate glass, known as Pyrex, is heat resistant. Heat-resistant glass does not break like regular glass, which allows chemists to heat samples and then rapidly cool them without having glass shatter all over their labs.

Discovery Zone Borax was used and known about for many years. It came from the Tibet region of China and was used to purify gold (#79) from the ore dug up by miners. In 1808, three famous scientists—Joseph-Louis Gay-Lussac, Louis Jacques Thénard, and Sir Humphry Davy—collected boron by heating borax with potassium (#19). Gay-Lussac and Thénard worked together, while Davy worked separately. Boron is so reactive that it was not until 100 years later, in 1909, that Ezekiel Weintraub was able to collect totally pure boron.

BORON

CARBON

Carbon is the 15th most abundant element in the earth's crust, but it is probably the most important element to you (even if you didn't know it until now). About 20% of your total body is made of carbon, making you—like all humans—a carbon-based life-form.

Carbon is in both pencil "leads" (no lead in there!) and diamonds, which are both made up of only carbon. Carbon in pencils is the graphite form and is pretty soft. The diamond form of carbon, though, is the hardest mineral we know. We knew all about carbon for thousands of years, but humans did not discover the third form of carbon until the 1980s, when Richard Smalley, Robert Curl, and Harold Kroto discovered that carbon exists in soccer ball shapes consisting of 60 atoms. They named the new form of carbon after architect Buckminster Fuller. Yes, the official name of C_{60} is buckminsterfullerene!

Discovery Zone Carbon has been known for almost all of human history because of its many uses. It was named an element in 1789 by Antoine Lavoisier, using the Latin word *carbo* for charcoal or coal. We know of more than 10 billion different carbon-based molecules; not surprising, when you consider that there is a whole branch of chemistry—organic chemistry—focused solely on carbon!

ELEMENTAL STATS

P+ 6
E- 6
N 6

State: Solid

Atomic Mass: 12.01 amu

Density: 3.513 g/cm³

Atomic Radius: 170 pm

Element Group: Carbon Family

CARBON

ELEMENTAL STATS

P+ 7
E- 7
N 7

State: Gas

Atomic Mass:
14.01 amu

Density:
0.0012506 g/mL

Atomic Radius:
65 pm

Element Group:
Pnictogens

NITROGEN

N itrogen is the fifth most abundant element on Earth and is 78% of what you are breathing right now. However, you could not breathe nitrogen on its own.

While nitrogen gas is odorless and colorless, we convert it into many different forms, relying on compounds of nitrogen to survive. The Haber–Bosch process, an industrial process, changes nitrogen (N_2) gas into ammonia (NH_3) gas. Almost 2% of all of the world's energy supply goes into this conversion. We use the ammonia to make fertilizers so we can grow more plants more quickly to feed our animals and ourselves. Yet, there are amazing **enzymes** in nature that convert nitrogen into ammonia, and smart people all around the world are working to duplicate this feat so we can make ammonia without using so much energy.

Nitrogen is needed in all plants and animals and is built into our proteins and DNA. If we didn't have nitrogen, we couldn't have DNA. Without DNA, there would be no life.

Discovery Zone A number of scientists studied nitrogen without realizing that they were studying a new element. Scientists such as Henry Cavendish and Joseph Priestley thought they were working with "burnt air," not a new element. However, in 1772, Daniel Rutherford realized that nitrogen was indeed an element, and named it after the common mineral called niter, a compound that contains the element.

NITROGEN

OXYGEN

Where would we be without oxygen? Oxygen really is the breath of life. It helps our bodies remove the extra electrons we release when we turn food into energy, water, and carbon dioxide. However, many people are surprised to learn that oxygen is not the biggest part of the air we breathe. It makes up only about 21%, and the rest is mostly nitrogen (#7). Oxygen is found in many molecules and compounds, making it the most abundant element in the planet's crust.

Firefighters use oxygen tanks when working around burning buildings so they can breathe and revive people and animals. Oxygen is also needed in transportation, as most cars, buses, and planes still burn a fuel like gasoline to make the engines go. During the burning process (combustion), oxygen reacts with the gasoline fuel, giving us energy, heat, water, and carbon dioxide. We use the heat and energy to move the vehicles and release the water and carbon dioxide in the process.

 Discovery Zone Three people are commonly given credit for discovering oxygen: Joseph Priestley, Antoine Lavoisier, and Carl Wilhelm Scheele. The credit often goes to Priestley because he was the first to publish his observation that oxygen was released after heating mercuric oxide, HgO. An important part of any scientist's activities is sharing their results through writings or presentations so that other scientists can study their new ideas (and give them credit for being first).

ELEMENTAL STATS

P+ 8
E- 8
N 8

State: Gas

Atomic Mass: 15.99 amu

Density: 0.001308 g/mL

Atomic Radius: 152 pm

Element Group: Chalcogens

OXYGEN

ELEMENTAL STATS

P+ 9
E- 9
N 10

State: Gas

Atomic Mass:
18.99 amu

Density:
0.001553 g/mL

Atomic Radius:
147 pm

Element Group:
Halogens

FLUORINE

Do you ever get tired of being told to brush your teeth? Your parents are trying to help you protect your teeth. The fluoride in toothpaste makes your teeth stronger, preventing cavities. Fluoride (F^-) is the negatively charged form of fluorine. You will find it in your toothpaste as sodium fluoride (NaF), which is safer and less reactive.

Fluorine (the neutral atom) is the most reactive element in the periodic table and will react with nearly every other element. Reactions with fluorine can be sudden and explosive. You have to keep it separated from other materials, since it strongly wants to gain another electron (and is in fact the most **electronegative** element, pulling electrons toward itself). It exists in nature as F_2, a diatomic (two-atom) gas, and is the 13th most common element in the earth's crust. The main source of fluorine is CaF_2, or fluorspar (fluorite), a beautiful crystal.

Discovery Zone We now know that fluorine is an element in the halogen family, meaning that it behaves a lot like the other halogens, such as chlorine (#17). This similarity was the key to chemists' first collection of fluorine, but it also made it a challenge. Many chemists tried to isolate the new halogen, but it was not until 1869, when George Gore electrified hydrogen fluoride, that fluorine was found in its pure form as a gas. By the way, Gore destroyed most of his tools in the process, as the newly made fluorine reacted with all the metal tools around it.

FLUORINE

NEON

Neon is a gas. When placed inside a tube and heated, it emits a bright red glow. Today, neon lights seem to be everywhere and are great for eye-catching business signs. Being a noble gas, neon is not very reactive, unlike its neighbor fluorine (#9). Neon does not undergo chemical reactions as a noble gas, so you will not find compounds containing neon in any products at a store.

Discovery Zone After Mendeleev gave chemists the periodic table, they soon realized that there were "missing" elements yet to be discovered. To hunt some of the missing elements, William Ramsay and Morris Travers slowly heated samples of liquid air. They studied the gases that boiled off, which allowed them to discover not just neon but also krypton (#36)! Neon was placed into their atomic spectrometer, surprising the scientists with the red glow we are now used to seeing in neon signs.

ELEMENTAL STATS

P+ 10
E- 10
N 10

State: Gas

Atomic Mass:
20.18 amu

Density:
0.000825 g/mL

Atomic Radius:
154 pm

Element Group:
Noble Gases

NEON

SODIUM

ELEMENTAL STATS

P+ 11
E- 11
N 12

State: Solid

Atomic Mass:
22.99 amu

Density:
0.97 g/cm³

Atomic Radius:
227 pm

Element Group:
Alkali Metals

Sodium is one of the most important elements to us, and not just because sodium chloride, the stuff we call "salt," is great on French fries and pretzels! Without sodium as Na⁺, our muscles wouldn't work properly.

Sodium is an alkali metal in the first column of the periodic table and is the sixth most abundant element in Earth's crust. It reacts rapidly with water to lose an electron to form Na⁺. Sodium metal also reacts with the halogen family to make salts like sodium chloride (NaCl), which is one sodium and one chlorine (#17) combined together to make table salt.

Have you ever noticed that your sweat tastes salty? That's because when you sweat, you are releasing sodium (as sodium chloride) from your body. For us to move around and control our muscles, we need sodium ions, Na⁺. Most of the sodium ions in our body are outside our cells. For our muscles to operate the right way, the passageways in the cell membrane must open, allowing sodium to rush in. If someone works out so hard that they sweat a lot, their muscles may start twitching on their own. To avoid this twitchy situation, serious athletes will drink sports drinks, which are saltwater with coloring and some sugar. The drinks give their bodies water and more NaCl to prevent muscles from shaking.

 Discovery Zone Sir Humphry Davy discovered sodium in 1807. He was a famous electrochemist and, true to form, used electricity to discover sodium. He was trying to prove that caustic soda (sodium hydroxide, or NaOH) was an oxidized metal. Davy sent electrical currents through the NaOH, breaking the oxygen (#8) off and leaving the pure metal, sodium. While the English name for sodium comes from a word meaning "headache remedy," its symbol, Na, comes from a Latin word, *natrium,* for a sodium-containing compound, sodium carbonate.

SODIUM

MAGNESIUM

Magnesium is the eighth most abundant element in Earth's crust and has a variety of uses in nature and in industry. It is a very lightweight metal that is often mixed with metals like aluminum (#13) to be used in cars and planes. You have most likely seen magnesium during celebrations such as the Fourth of July. A brightly glowing sparkler is actually magnesium metal on a stick burning with oxygen (#8). Be careful with those sparklers, as they burn bright *and* hot!

Maybe even more remarkable is how nature uses magnesium. A magnesium ion sits at the center of a chlorophyll molecule, giving us green grass and leaves. If your garden plants aren't as green as they should be, you can add Epsom salts (magnesium sulfate, or $MgSO_4$) to provide the magnesium that plants need to make chlorophyll. And as it turns out, Epsom salts also help scratches and rashes heal more quickly—an observation first made in 1618 by a farmer.

 Discovery Zone Joseph Black first realized that magnesium was an element distinct from calcium (#20) in 1755. Calcium is in the same column as magnesium, and it is chemically very similar, but Black observed that minerals of calcium dissolved in water differently than those of magnesium. However, it was not until 1808 that Humphry Davy was able to collect pure magnesium using electrical methods.

ELEMENTAL STATS

P+ 12
E- 12
N 12

State: Solid

Atomic Mass: 24.31 amu

Density: 1.74 g/cm³

Atomic Radius: 173 pm

Element Group: Alkaline Earth Metals

MAGNESIUM

ELEMENTAL STATS

P+ 13
E- 13
N 14

State: Solid

Atomic Mass:
26.98 amu

Density:
2.70 g/cm³

Atomic Radius:
184 pm

Element Group:
Boron Family

ALUMINUM

Aluminum is a lightweight metal, similar to magnesium (#12), but it is used even more since it is less reactive than magnesium. Almost everyone has used aluminum foil, and aluminum cans filled with soda pop and sparkling water are everywhere. Aluminum is even used to make trucks and planes lighter in weight. Because aluminum is used in so many ways, you might not be surprised to learn that it is the most abundant metal on Earth and the third most abundant element in Earth's crust.

Aluminum, which was first shown to the public at the Paris Exposition of 1855, was only used by the very rich before 1886. That's because while aluminum minerals are everywhere, removing aluminum from the bauxite mineral takes a lot of effort and energy. It was a big deal when Charles Martin Hall developed a better method using electricity to purify aluminum in 1886. He went on to start the Aluminum Company of America, known as Alcoa, introducing cheap aluminum to the world. But purifying aluminum still takes a lot of energy, so you can do your part in making our world sustainable by recycling your aluminum cans.

Discovery Zone In 1825, Hans Christian Ørsted heated aluminum chloride with potassium (#19) in Denmark, producing the first sample of aluminum. Unfortunately, it was not pure; German chemist Friedrich Wöhler was the first to obtain a pure sample of aluminum in 1827.

ALUMINUM

SILICON

Silicon is the seventh most abundant element in the universe and the second most abundant element in Earth's crust. Silicon is similar to carbon (#6) in that it often makes four bonds and, like carbon, can make bonds with itself.

If you remember, carbon's ability to connect to itself is one of the reasons we are carbon-based life forms. Well, because silicon can also make bonds with itself and is so abundant in the universe, scientists have wondered if alien life might be silicon-based and not carbon-based.

But you are more likely to run into silicon atoms when you get to the beach and see white sand (silicon with two oxygens, or SiO_2). White sand is a compound of silicon and oxygen (#8) that is the remnants of algae. Of course, you get to use silicon every day because your phones and computers are powered by silicon chips. So, thank silicon for our modern world!

 Discovery Zone In 1787, Antoine Lavoisier suggested that sand (SiO_2) was an element. But years later, while Humphry Davy was studying elements, he found out that sand was a compound. And it was years after that before Jöns Jacob Berzelius was finally able to collect pure silicon.

ELEMENTAL STATS

P+ 14
E- 14
N 14

State: Solid

Atomic Mass:
28.09 amu

Density:
2.33 g/cm³

Atomic Radius:
210 pm

Element Group:
Carbon Family

SILICON

ELEMENTAL STATS

P+ 15
E- 15
N 16

State: Solid

Atomic Mass: 30.97 amu

Density: White 1.823 g/cm³

Atomic Radius: 180 pm

Element Group: Pnictogens

PHOSPHORUS

The 11th most abundant element, phosphorus, is used in our bodies in several ways. As phosphate (PO_4^{3-}), it holds DNA molecules together, making all life possible. In the human body, phosphorus binds with calcium (#20) to make strong bones and teeth. In fact, most of the phosphorus in our bodies is found in our teeth and bones, but it's not in its elemental form. Rather, it is in a form called hydroxyapatite.

It's not just humans that need phosphorus. Because all DNA needs phosphorus and all living things have DNA, phosphorus is used as a component of the fertilizer you can use to help a garden grow.

Phosphorus is also a diverse element, like carbon (#6). As it turns out, there are actually four elemental forms of phosphorus: red, white, violet, and black. Chemists have a special name for different forms of an element: **allotropes**.

Discovery Zone Because phosphorus is a component of DNA, we already know that phosphorus is vital to life. So maybe you aren't too surprised to learn that the discoverer of phosphorus, Hennig Brand, collected it from urine in 1669. It took another 100 years for scientists to discover that they could also obtain pure phosphorus from bones.

PHOSPHORUS

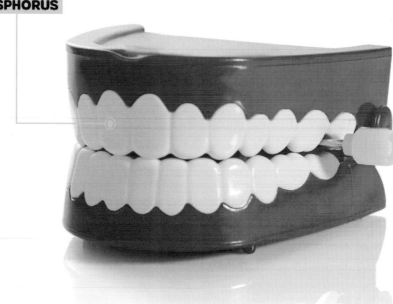

SULFUR

Sulfur is stinky. There's no other way to describe it. If you have ever been near skunk spray, then you *know* sulfur. Besides being part of a defense spray in skunks, there are a lot of good uses for sulfur.

Industrially, sulfur may be the most used element—not bad for the 17th most abundant element in Earth's crust. The process of vulcanizing rubber (which involves adding sulfur) was invented by Charles Goodyear in 1839 and is used to make rubber stronger, giving us safer tires. Sulfur is also used to make sulfuric acid (H_2SO_4), a chemical in many important substances, such as detergents, dyes, and medicines. More importantly, sulfuric acid is needed to make phosphates (#15), key ingredients in the fertilizers that farmers use to ensure good crops.

Discovery Zone Sulfur has been known since antiquity, but we didn't understand it to be an element for many years. It has been known for so long that it is mentioned in the Bible. Eventually, in the 1770s, Antoine Lavoisier convinced other scientists that sulfur was an element during his experiments with air.

ELEMENTAL STATS

P+ 16
E- 16
N 16

State: Solid

Atomic Mass: 32.06 amu

Density: 2.07 g/cm³

Atomic Radius: 180 pm

Element Group: Chalcogens

SULFUR

CHLORINE

State: Gas

Atomic Mass: 35.45 amu

Density: 0.00290 g/cm³

Atomic Radius: 175 pm

Element Group: Halogens

You will encounter chlorine every time you go swimming because it is added to swimming pool water to kill off harmful bacteria. Many water systems use chlorine gas to kill bacteria so you can drink microbe-free water. This should also tell you that chlorine gas is dangerous. You do not want to breathe elemental chlorine gas. Fortunately, it only takes a little bit to kill harmful microbes, so have fun swimming. Chlorine is a yellow-green colored gas, so its name makes sense if you know Greek because *chloros* is Greek for a green-yellow color.

About 20% of the chlorine produced is used to make polyvinyl-chloride (PVC) piping. PVC piping is used for plumbing and drainage, so check out the piping under your sink. If it is a white plastic, it is most likely PVC. And don't forget the salt on your French fries is sodium chloride, NaCl. The *–ide* ending of "chloride" tells scientists that chlorine has grabbed an electron to become a negatively charged ion, an **anion**.

Sodium chloride is one of the most important seasonings and obviously not dangerous like pure chlorine. Humans have used salt to make food taste better all around the world for a long time. Salt has also spurred human exploration and helped build connections between countries.

Discovery Zone Elemental chlorine, Cl₂, was first collected by Carl Wilhelm Scheele in 1774. He added hydrochloric acid (HCl) to the mineral pyrolusite, creating a yellow-green gas. In these early stages of chemistry, scientists did not often realize the importance or meaning of their discoveries. Scheele did not know what he had discovered until Humphry Davy came along and argued in 1810 that the gas was an element. And scientists being scientists (they need good evidence), it took another 10 years before chlorine was accepted as an element.

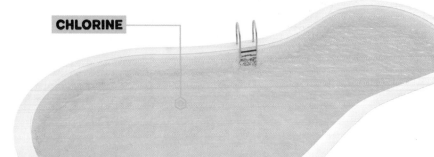

CHLORINE

ARGON

In 1785, Henry Cavendish realized that about 1% of the air would not react, confusing and frustrating him. So he gave the unreactive part of air a special name—argon. The name comes from the Greek word *argos*, meaning "lazy" or "inactive."

It was much later before the colorless and odorless gas argon was isolated and beautiful light from the gas was observed. Argon is one of our noble gases, so it is no surprise that the gas does not react; it simply hides in the air we breathe, even though it is the third most abundant gas in our air.

In addition to being used for lighting in lamps, argon creates an unreactive space in which to do chemistry. Welders also use argon to protect their metals as they heat them because the argon blankets the metal so oxygen (#8) can't get to it. Without argon, a lot of metals would react with the oxygen in the air and start rusting.

 Discovery Zone Because argon is unreactive, it is very good at hiding in plain sight. It was not until 1894 that it was isolated. Lord Rayleigh and William Ramsay separated it from liquid air. To get argon, first nitrogen (#7), oxygen, carbon dioxide, and water had to be removed from air. The remaining residue gave them the hiding argon gas. Their experiment essentially replicated a method devised by another scientist, Henry Cavendish, for separating elements in the air.

ELEMENTAL STATS

P+ 18
E- 18
N 22

State: Gas

Atomic Mass: 39.95 amu

Density: 0.00163 g/mL

Atomic Radius: 188 pm

Element Group: Noble Gases

ARGON

POTASSIUM

ELEMENTAL STATS

P+ 19
E- 19
N 20

State: Solid

Atomic Mass:
39.10 amu

Density:
0.862 g/cm³

Atomic Radius:
275 pm

Element Group:
Alkali Metals

Potassium is the seventh most abundant element in Earth's crust, which is a good thing because both humans and plants need it. Like sodium (#11), our bodies need potassium to make muscles move. The movement of muscles begins when potassium ions enter a cell, allowing a message to be sent to the cell. The potassium must then be pumped back out of the cell so the next signal can be sent. Most of the potassium we need is used in our cells, but some potassium is also needed for good bone health. That's why nutritionists recommend you eat foods high in potassium, such as bananas and spinach.

I hope you are not tired of fertilizer yet, because just like nitrogen (#7) and phosphorus (#15), potassium is important for plant growth. While the largest use of potassium is in fertilizers, potassium is also used in saponification, the process of making soaps, which we need to keep us healthy. Potassium hydroxide (KOH), or lye, is added to fats, the gooey stuff from plants or animals, to make soap.

Discovery Zone Potassium is never found as the pure element in nature because it is very reactive. Yet in 1807, Humphry Davy was able to collect the metal using electricity (as he did with sodium, calcium [#20], boron [#5], strontium [#38], and magnesium [#12]), kick-starting his celebrity career, both as a scientist and with the public.

POTASSIUM

CALCIUM

Calcium is the fifth most abundant element in Earth's crust, and you probably know that we need it for healthy bodies. You may recall your parents telling you to drink your milk so you can get enough calcium for your growing bones and teeth. The element calcium is very different from the calcium compound in your bones. It is a silvery-colored, alkaline earth metal that reacts in air and water to form more stable calcium ions, Ca^{2+}. It is the ion that combines with materials in our bones to make them stronger.

Seashells are made out of calcium carbonate—pretty much rock. Its hardness is important for protecting the sea creatures living inside the shells. Even more amazing are coccolithophores, plants that surround themselves with plates of calcium carbonate armor. The next time you are walking on the beach, think about all the calcium around you.

Humans use calcium compounds to make concrete and plaster to build bridges and walls. As the building block for many materials that make our lives possible, calcium is a very useful element.

 Discovery Zone In the 1700s, Antoine Lavoisier thought of lime (calcium oxide or CaO) as an "earth," since he could not break it into anything smaller. It took Humphry Davy many attempts and heating lots of lime with mercury (#80) compounds to obtain pure calcium in 1808.

ELEMENTAL STATS

P+ 20
E- 20
N 20

State: Solid

Atomic Mass:
40.08 amu

Density:
1.54 g/cm³

Atomic Radius:
231 pm

Element Group:
Alkaline Earth Metals

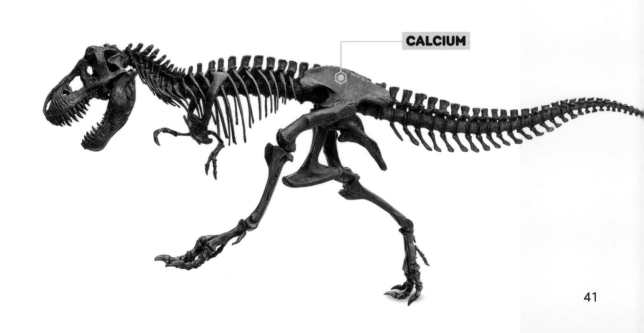

CALCIUM

SCANDIUM

ELEMENTAL STATS

P+ 21
E- 21
N 23

State: Solid

Atomic Mass:
44.96 amu

Density:
2.99 g/cm³

Atomic Radius:
215 pm

Element Group:
Transition Metal

Scandium is the first metal of a new section of the periodic table: the transition metals. While scandium is not rare, as the 35th most abundant element in Earth's crust, it doesn't exist in large quantities in very many spots. The element is spread out all over the place, making it difficult to collect and expensive to buy. You would pay about $2,000 for a pound of scandium, a lot more than the $2 you would pay for a pound of apples.

The high cost of scandium makes it tough to put it to good use. Yet, researchers have mixed a small amount of scandium with aluminum (#13) to make the metal frames of bicycles and planes. The new mixed metal is lighter than and about twice as strong as just aluminum itself. Scientists have also mixed a compound of scandium (scandium iodide) to make lights that create a "whiter" light indoors, helping our gyms to feel more like the outdoors.

Discovery Zone Have you ever heard of Scandinavia? It is the name given to the region that includes Denmark, Norway, and Sweden. Think scandium sounds a lot like Scandinavia? Well, it is named after the region. Lars Fredrik Nilson discovered and named the element in 1879. At the time, he was actually trying to purify another element, ytterbium (#70), from a pile of minerals from Scandinavia.

SCANDIUM

TITANIUM

While titanium is the ninth most abundant element in Earth's crust, it rarely exists as a pure metal. Titanium is a very strong but light metal. It is as strong as steel but weighs a lot less. This makes it great for making alloys (mixtures of two metals).

Alloys containing titanium are used for making aircraft, spaceships, and rockets because they are lightweight and heat resistant. Titanium is also corrosion resistant, meaning that it does not rust easily. This makes titanium great for building boats and for making pipes to carry fresh water and seawater. Titanium plates have also been used to construct cool-looking buildings like the Guggenheim Bilbao museum in Spain.

Around your home, you might find titanium in golf clubs, computers, and even in your bicycle. You might also find it in your mouth! Titanium connects well with bone and teeth, so bone and tooth implants often use titanium. Titanium oxides, compounds made with titanium and oxygen (#8), are used in many sunscreens to reflect the harmful parts of sunlight away from your skin and protect you from sunburns.

 Discovery Zone In 1791, William Gregor discovered a new element, naming it manaccanite to honor the Manaccan valley where he found the mineral. A few years later, in 1795, Martin Heinrich Klaproth was studying the mineral schörl when he decided it was made up of oxygen and some new element. Klaproth called his new element titanium. To check his work on the new element, Klaproth studied Gregor's work and confirmed they were the same metal. Sadly for Gregor, Klaproth's name stuck even though Klaproth admitted that Gregor had discovered it. And in 1910, Matthew Albert Hunter was finally able to make pure titanium.

ELEMENTAL STATS

P+ 22
E- 22
N 26

State: Solid

Atomic Mass: 47.87 amu

Density: 4.51 g/cm³

Atomic Radius: 211 pm

Element Group: Transition Metals

TITANIUM

VANADIUM

State: Solid

Atomic Mass:
50.94 amu

Density:
6.0 g/cm³

Atomic Radius:
207 pm

Element Group:
Transition
Metals

Have you ever heard of a sea squirt? They go by the scientific name ascidians. They are pretty amazing sea creatures because they collect vanadium as it flows past them in sea water. There is only a small amount of vanadium in water, but sea squirts have a lot of this element in their bodies. Many scientists think these creatures use the vanadium to get oxygen (#8) to their cells in the same way that mammals use iron (#26).

This pure gray silvery metal is not found by itself in nature—it is always combined with another element. It can be removed from the compounds and used to make alloys by mixing with other metals. Vanadium steel is made by mixing this element with iron to make a stronger steel. This is often used for tank armor and car and truck parts. More than 80% of purified vanadium is added to steel. Vanadium is also alloyed with aluminum (#13) and titanium (#22) to create a very strong material used for jet engines. Vanadium can form toxic compounds when combined with other elements, so it should be handled carefully.

VANADIUM

Discovery Zone
In 1801, Andrés Manuel del Río, while studying minerals in Mexico City, discovered a new element that made many different colored compounds. He named his new element erythronium. Unfortunately, chemists back in Europe did not believe him, and his conclusions were ignored. Then, in 1831, Nils Gabriel Sefström collected a new element from cast iron and named it vanadium, after a Scandinavian goddess of beauty. It turns out that it was the same metal that del Río had found. Thirty years later, pure vanadium was finally collected by Henry Roscoe.

CHROMIUM

Chromium is used to make a lot of colored materials. One of the most popular colors made from chromium is yellow. You may call it "school bus yellow," but the color of school buses is known as chrome yellow. Chromium also makes a lot of beautifully colored compounds. Chromium (III) oxide is green, lead chromate is yellow, chromium (III) chloride is purple, and chromium trioxide is red. The "III" after the element name means that the chromium in this particular compound has given away three electrons.

Even though it is used to make various colors, pure chromium is a hard, shiny metal. Stainless steel is a combination of chromium and steel. Stainless steel is strong and not easily destroyed, making it useful for silverware and sinks. Chromium is also mixed with nickel (#28) to make jet engines. From your kitchen to jet planes, chromium is all around you.

 Discovery Zone In 1798, Nicolas-Louis Vauquelin was studying a colored mineral collected from a gold mine to figure out what elements it contained. He thought it was a lead (#82) mineral with other stuff in it. When he added a liquid acid to the mineral and removed the undissolved lead, the new element emerged from the liquid. He named it chromium from the Greek word *chroma*, meaning "color," because of the many different colors the element made in solutions with other elements.

ELEMENTAL STATS

P+ 24
E- 24
N 28

State: Solid

Atomic Mass: 52 amu

Density: 7.15 g/cm³

Atomic Radius: 206 pm

Element Group: Transition Metals

CHROMIUM

25

Mn

ELEMENTAL STATS

P+ 25
E- 25
N 30

State: Solid

Atomic Mass:
54.94 amu

Density:
7.3 g/cm³

Atomic Radius:
205 pm

Element Group:
Transition Metals

MANGANESE

Manganese is the fifth most abundant metal in Earth's crust, but it is so reactive that it is mainly found in minerals, usually with its periodic-table neighbor—iron (#26). It is not useful as a metal on its own, but when combined with steel, it makes a very strong material, usable for prison bars and railroad tracks.

Manganese also makes many different colors, such as manganese violet, a compound in makeup. You may have used manganese combined with oxygen (#8), known as manganese dioxide (MnO_2). In this form, it is an important part of your standard store-bought batteries, called dry cell batteries.

More importantly, manganese atoms in plants are needed to turn water into oxygen during photosynthesis—using the energy gathered by chlorophyll, containing magnesium (#12) ions—so plants can survive.

 Discovery Zone Pyrolusite, or MnO_2, was apparently the black coloring used in prehistoric times for cave drawings, but manganese metal was much more difficult to collect. While other chemists had previously tried to isolate it, Swedish chemist Johan Gottlieb Gahn was the first to be successful in 1774. When he heated pyrolusite in charcoal, the reaction produced the element manganese for the first time.

MANGANESE

IRON

26

Fe

Iron is one of the most crucial elements to humans. Unfortunately, pure iron undergoes oxidation pretty easily; in other words, it rusts! But humans learned to make what today is the most common type of steel by combining iron with carbon (#6). Steel is used everywhere, from buildings to tools. But that's not all. In fact, you can thank iron for life itself!

You are breathing in oxygen (#8) at this very moment. You need the oxygen to survive, but iron moves the oxygen from the air all the way to your cells. At the center of each of your red blood cells sits an iron atom. The iron atom can grab onto an oxygen molecule and hold onto it gently. The iron in your red blood cells then carries the oxygen to all the cells in your body. Those red blood cells then go right back to your lungs to get more oxygen, repeating this transportation process over and over.

Discovery Zone People have known about iron for so long that no one scientist is given credit for its discovery. Iron was so important to old civilizations that historians named a whole era after the element: the "Iron Age." Some historians think that this time period began as many as 10,000 years ago—well before any scientists were writing down and publishing their discoveries.

ELEMENTAL STATS

P+ 26
E- 26
N 30

State: Solid

Atomic Mass: 55.85 amu

Density: 7.87 g/cm³

Atomic Radius: 204 pm

Element Group: Transition Metals

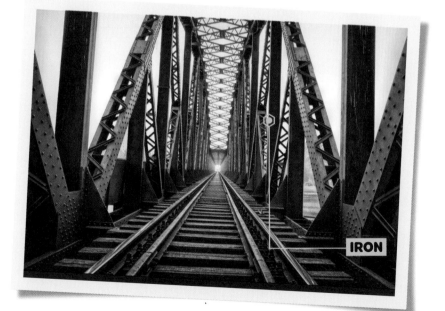

IRON

ELEMENTAL STATS

P+ 27
E- 27
N 32

State: Solid

Atomic Mass:
58.93 amu

Density:
8.86 g/cm³

Atomic Radius:
200 pm

Element Group:
Transition
Metals

COBALT

on't be blue for cobalt; cobalt is already blue. Cobalt makes a lot of blue colors and is used to brightly color jewelry, paints, and glass. People even named a shade of blue after the element—cobalt blue. Yet cobalt is also used to make **pigments** such as cobalt yellow and cobalt green. Cobalt is also an important component of vitamin B_{12}, which helps keep our blood cells healthy and helps in the DNA-making process.

Unfortunately, German miners did not like finding cobalt ores while digging for silver (#47) and nickel (#28) because it meant that they would have to separate the elements in the ores. Aside from the extra work, there was another reason for their dislike of cobalt. Miners nicknamed cobalt ores "kobold," or goblin ore, because miners would get sick and sometimes die when working with the cobalt ores. At the time, they didn't know exactly why this was happening. It turns out that cobalt is often found in combination with arsenic (#33), a poison, as cobaltite. When they heated the cobalt ores to extract the silver and nickel, a toxic gas would be released from the cobaltite.

Discovery Zone While we know that cobalt gives many materials a blue color, before the discovery of this element, many scientists thought the blue color came from bismuth (#83). However, Georg Brandt did not believe this and set out to isolate the material he thought made the blue hue. He proved cobalt was a new element and different from bismuth through six different tests, looking at properties like melting points and stiffness.

COBALT

NICKEL

Nickel has many uses, like speeding up the **hydrogenation** of vegetable oils. We add hydrogen (#1) to vegetable oil to make it less of a liquid and more "solid-like," which allows the food to last longer and keep its flavor. Nickel is used as a catalyst in hydrogenation. Not bad for a metal you may have only thought of as a coin!

While nickel is a coinage metal, like silver (#47), gold (#79), and copper (#29), the United States nickel coin contains only 25% nickel. The rest of it is copper. Dimes and quarters contain nickel, too; a little more than 8% of those coins are nickel. Besides coins, stainless-steel knives, forks, and spoons also contain this element. Nickel keeps those utensils from rusting (as in *stainless*!).

Most of the nickel on Earth is believed to have been brought here by meteors. So, there is reason to be thankful for meteors!

 Discovery Zone In 1751, Swedish chemist Axel Fredrik Cronstedt collected an impure form of nickel from the mineral niccolite (NiAs). He was studying the red-colored mineral because miners thought it contained copper but could not extract Cu from it. Turns out there was no copper in the ore, but a new element—nickel—was found.

ELEMENTAL STATS

P+ 28
E- 28
N 31

State: Solid

Atomic Mass: 58.69 amu

Density: 8.90 g/cm³

Atomic Radius: 197 pm

Element Group: Transition Metals

NICKEL

COPPER

ELEMENTAL STATS

P+ 29
E- 29
N 34 or 35

State: Solid

Atomic Mass: 63.55 amu

Density: 8.96 g/cm³

Atomic Radius: 196 pm

Element Group: Transition Metals

Copper may be the first metal mined and used by humans. There is evidence that we have been working with copper for more than 10,000 years. Copper is great, but bronze is even stronger, making it a great material for making shields and weapons. Bronze is two parts copper and one part tin (#50). The production of bronze led people from the Stone Age to a more advanced civilization, the Bronze Age.

Copper is also a great conductor of electricity and is used in wires to carry electricity all over the world. Today, we also mix copper with gold (#79) to make pink gold for jewelry.

Copper and nickel (#28) are used to make the United States penny. Copper has been used for money in many different countries for thousands of years. You can also roof your house with copper (although this might prove to be a bit expensive) or wrap a statue with it, like the Statue of Liberty. Lady Liberty is not reddish like the element. Rather, she has a greenish look. That's because of the reaction between copper and other elements in the environment.

 Discovery Zone Copper is considered one of the prehistoric elements. No one kept a record of who found it first or added their name to it. We do know, however, that it was used at least 10,000 years ago, as we have dug up copper beads from ancient civilizations!

COPPER

ZINC

Most people hanging out in the sunshine may not be thinking of zinc, but maybe they should be. Zinc oxide, along with titanium dioxide, is a key ingredient in our sunscreens. The white metal can protect us from sunburn and other damage by reflecting the sun. Humans have known about and used zinc for thousands of years, and not just to avoid sunburns.

If you are a musician, or just a music-lover, you know brass instruments such as the tuba and trumpet. Brass is a mixture (or alloy) of zinc and copper (#29). A lot of the zinc made is used to coat metals like iron (#26) to prevent corrosion—a process called **galvanization**. We also use compounds like zinc sulfide (ZnS) to make our watches glow.

Zinc is not only useful; it's also essential. All living things require zinc. More than 20 enzymes in your body need zinc to work correctly.

 Discovery Zone Humans have known about zinc for thousands of years, but it appears that elemental zinc was first collected in India. Way back in the 1400s, calamine ($ZnCO_3$) was heated with wool, producing zinc metal. It was discovered in the western world in 1746 by Andreas Sigismund Marggraf, who heated the same mineral with charcoal.

ELEMENTAL STATS

P+ 30
E- 30
N 35

State: Solid

Atomic Mass: 65.38 amu

Density: 7.13 g/cm³

Atomic Radius: 201 pm

Element Group: Transition Metals

ZINC

31
Ga

ELEMENTAL STATS

P+ 31
E- 31
N 39

State: Solid

Atomic Mass:
69.72 amu

Density:
5.91 g/cm³

Atomic Radius:
187 pm

Element Group:
Boron Family

GALLIUM

Gallium is not found in its elemental form on Earth. It hangs around with zinc (#30) and aluminum (#13), and they are often found together in Earth's crust. Purified gallium metal has a low melting point (30°C)—so it could melt in your hand! Gallium stays liquid for the longest time of any element. Water boils at 100°C, while gallium boils at 2400°C.

It is also quite reactive and will react with acids and bases to form other compounds. Gallium compounds like GaN and GaAs are used in semiconductors to make solar panels, light-emitting diodes (LEDs), and mobile phones. Since a lot of people use their smartphones every day, you might have some gallium in your pocket (or hand!) right now.

Discovery Zone A Frenchman, Paul-Émile Lecoq de Boisbaudran, discovered gallium in 1875, so maybe you will understand why the name comes from the Latin name for France. Boisbaudran's specialty was spectroscopy (using light to study the elements), which helped him discover not only gallium but also samarium (#62), europium (#63), and dysprosium (#66).

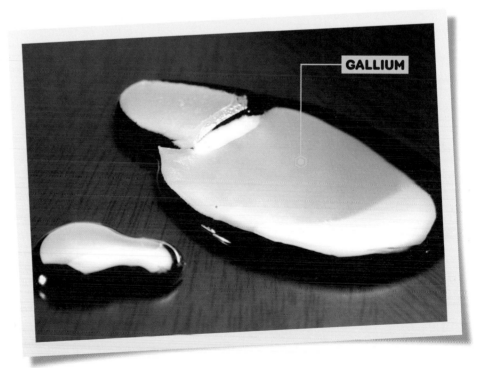

GALLIUM

GERMANIUM

Germanium is a pretty flower, right? No, that's a geranium. Germanium is a rare element found in Earth's crust that has metal and nonmetal qualities.

It is a semiconductor like gallium (#31) and has electrical conductivity somewhere between an insulator (rubber) and a conductor (copper metal). Semiconductors are used in the electronics industry to make computers and cell phones. GeO_2 is transparent to light, like glass, and is used in microscopes and camera lenses. Because germanium is so rare, it has been mostly replaced by silicon (#14), which is found in sand.

 Discovery Zone Dmitri Mendeleev predicted the existence of germanium after organizing the periodic table. A number of chemists were eager to find the "missing element," but it could not be found until 1886, when Clemens A. Winkler first isolated it. The element was found in the mineral argyrodite. As Winkler was from Germany, he honored his home country by naming his discovery germanium.

ELEMENTAL STATS

P+ 32
E- 32
N 41

State: Solid

Atomic Mass: 72.64 amu

Density: 5.32 g/cm³

Atomic Radius: 211 pm

Element Group: Carbon Family

GERMANIUM

33
As

ELEMENTAL STATS

P+ 33
E- 33
N 42

State: Solid

Atomic Mass:
74.92 amu

Density:
5.75 g/cm³

Atomic Radius:
185 pm

Element Group:
Pnictogens

ARSENIC

I expect you know that arsenic is not good for you (or for anyone). Unfortunately, humans have known that this element is a poison for a long time, even during the Roman Empire. Roman leaders enacted laws making it illegal to poison others with arsenic. But arsenic was still used. During the Renaissance, the Borgia family (right) rose to power through many methods, including adding arsenic to wine to remove unwanted rivals!

Fortunately, in 1836, chemist James Marsh, upset that some people were getting away with murder, developed a method to prove the presence of arsenic. With this new detection method, he put arsenic poisoning out of style.

Arsenic isn't all bad, however. Chemists have also found that arsenic can be used to make better semiconductors, like those in your phone, but don't worry—that arsenic is chemically locked up and only helps you surf the Web.

Discovery Zone Arsenic has been known around the world for many years. From the ancient Egyptians to Chinese naturalist Li Shizhen in the 1500s, people often used arsenic as a pesticide (bug killer). However, German alchemist and philosopher Albertus Magnus, better known by some as Saint Albert the Great, is given the credit for isolating the element in 1250.

SELENIUM

If you ever get dandruff, you may end up using a special kind of shampoo. Dandruff-fighting shampoos contain selenium sulfide, a chemical that kills the fungus that causes dandruff. And you can just wash it all away.

Selenium is also great for another reason. Selenium is helping us change from using coal and natural gas for energy to using more solar technology, which doesn't harm the environment. Selenium helps solar (photovoltaic) cells convert sunlight to electrical energy. Selenium's resistance to electron flow changes when illuminated (because it is photoconductive). This same property makes it an important part of photocopiers. So, next time you make a photocopy, be sure to thank selenium.

 Discovery Zone While trying to determine if there was an impurity in sulfuric acid from a factory product, Jöns Jacob Berzelius first isolated selenium in 1817. As we have studied the discoveries of different elements, have you noticed that a good number of elements were isolated by Swedes? Sweden developed a mining and **assaying** industry, which encouraged the study of minerals, leading to the study of new elements.

ELEMENTAL STATS

P+ 34
E- 34
N 45

State: Solid

Atomic Mass: 78.97 amu

Density: 4.81 g/cm³

Atomic Radius: 190 pm

Element Group: Chalcogens

SELENIUM

35

Br

ELEMENTAL STATS

P+ 35
E- 35
N 45

State: Liquid

Atomic Mass:
79.90 amu

Density:
3.10 g/cm³

Atomic Radius:
185 pm

Element Group:
Halogens

BROMINE

Bromine was first discovered in the ocean and is one of two liquids on the periodic table. Tyrian purple was a bromine dye extracted from a Mediterranean mollusk and used by Roman emperors. The color purple was always kept for royalty because it was difficult to create.

Bromine compounds were once used for lots of materials, such as those in fire extinguishers, **pharmaceuticals**, and pesticides, until people discovered that bromine breaks down the needed ozone in the stratosphere and can cause health problems. The production of bromine compounds has been dramatically reduced, and only a few approved uses are left for this element.

The few approved bromine-containing compounds include medical drugs such as heart medicines and sedatives (medications that help you sleep). Bromine is also used to speed up chemical reactions in the development of pharmaceuticals, reducing the time needed to make medications to treat sick patients.

Discovery Zone

Not to put too much pressure on you, but German chemist Carl Löwig discovered bromine by studying the water from a mineral spring before he even got to college. Because he was starting college and worked hard in his classes, he didn't have time to finish his studies on the new element. This allowed Frenchman Antoine-Jérôme Balard to present his findings before Löwig could complete and present his.

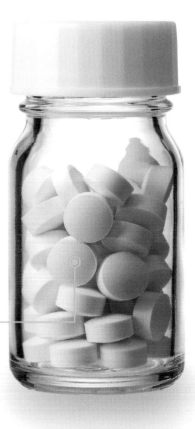

BROMINE

KRYPTON

First things first: There is no such element as kryptonite. Comic books want you to use your imagination, not necessarily learn chemistry. Yet krypton is a pretty cool element all on its own. It is a noble gas, meaning that it does not react easily with other elements.

The name *krypton* comes from the ancient Greek, meaning "hidden one." Many chemists struggled to identify and study this element. In the early 1900s, noble gases like neon (#10) and krypton amazed people with their colorful brightness, which made the shining lights in the big city a reality.

 Discovery Zone Krypton was discovered in 1898 by Sir William Ramsay and Morris Travers while they were studying liquefied air. Ramsay and Travers had to be good chemists to capture krypton on its own, as it makes up just one part per million of the air on Earth, meaning there is only one krypton atom in a million atoms of air.

ELEMENTAL STATS

P+ 36
E- 36
N 48

State: Gas

Atomic Mass:
83.80 amu

Density:
0.00343 g/mL

Atomic Radius:
202 pm

Element Group:
Noble Gases

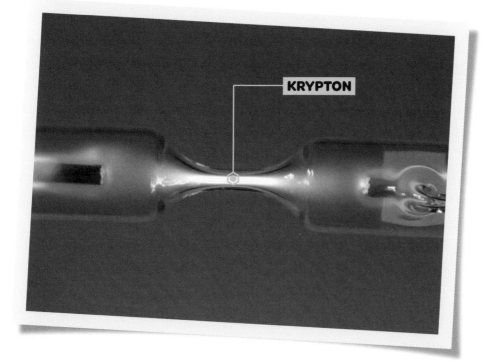

KRYPTON

State: Solid

Atomic Mass:
85.47 amu

Density:
1.53 g/cm³

Atomic Radius:
303 pm

Element Group:
Alkali Metals

RUBIDIUM

Surprisingly, there is not a lot of chemistry to talk about when it comes to rubidium. It is an alkali metal that reacts like potassium (#19) and cesium (#55). Like all alkali metals, rubidium easily loses an electron to become a rubidium ion (Rb⁺). Because of this property, NASA considered using the element for an ion engine in spacecraft. However, its alkali metal neighbor, cesium, worked better, as did the noble gas xenon (#54). One fun use of rubidium compounds is in fireworks, as rubidium nitrate, which is used to create a purple color.

Discovery Zone Robert Bunsen and Gustav Kirchhoff were studying the light from the mineral lepidolite in 1861 when they observed a deep-red color never seen before. They correctly deduced that the red color was caused by a new element, and they named the new element rubidium, for the Latin word *rubidius*, meaning "deepest red."

RUBIDIUM

STRONTIUM

When strontium salts burn, they emit a beautiful red color. If you have ever seen a flare burning on the side of the road to alert you of danger—possibly an accident—you are seeing strontium-emitting light. Strontium is not only used for flares, but is also a part of most Fourth of July celebrations, as it is used in fireworks.

Strontium is found in Earth's crust in compound form, not as the pure metal. Once purified, it is a silvery metal that reacts quickly with oxygen (#8). Besides the ones we've mentioned, there are not a whole lot of other uses for strontium compounds today. Strontium compounds were used in cathode-ray tubes in bulky, old-style televisions, but now we use semiconductors to make our flat-screen televisions.

Non-radioactive isotopes of strontium are used to treat people with low calcium levels. Interestingly, this element behaves a lot like calcium (#20) in your bones and helps strengthen them.

Discovery Zone Strontium was named after Strontian, a Scottish town where the rock containing the first strontium was found. Two men worked on discovering strontium. Adair Crawford first noticed that strontium ores were different from barium ores. Thomas Hope proved the difference by observing the elements in a flame. Strontium created a red flame, while barium (#56) made a green flame.

ELEMENTAL STATS

P+ 38
E- 38
N 50

State: Solid

Atomic Mass: 87.62 amu

Density: 2.64 g/cm³

Atomic Radius: 249 pm

Element Group: Alkaline Earth Metals

STRONTIUM

39
Y

ELEMENTAL STATS

P+ 39
E- 39
N 50

State: Solid

Atomic Mass:
88.91 amu

Density:
4.47 g/cm³

Atomic Radius:
232 pm

Element Group:
Transition
Metals

YTTRIUM

Yttrium is a transition metal, part of the middle block of the periodic table. It is also part of a group called rare earth metals. The rare earth metals (which are the lanthanides plus yttrium and scandium [#21]) are actually not that rare; they are about as abundant in Earth's crust as most other metals.

Yttrium compounds are widely used in high-tech equipment such as cell phones, display screens, lasers, and cell-phone towers. Yttrium lasers have been used for eye surgery and even tattoo removal.

Yttrium is also used in a high-tech tool called a **superconductor**. A superconductor is exactly what it sounds like—something that conducts electricity incredibly well. A superconductor made up of yttrium, barium (#56), copper (#29), and oxygen (#8) is one of the most studied superconductors. However, it only works at very cold temperatures. Scientists are doing research to make superconductors work at room temperature so we can save energy and create a greener world.

YTTRIUM

Discovery Zone Yttrium was discovered in a mineral from the town of Ytterby in Sweden, a famous element town. Four elements are named after it: yttrium, ytterbium (#70), erbium (#68), and terbium (#65)! The mineral that gave us yttrium was originally thought to be a tungsten (#74) ore, but analysis by Johan Gadolin revealed the new element. Remember Johan's name when we get to gadolinium (#64).

ZIRCONIUM

You may have some zirconium in your home and not even know it. Cubic zirconia (fake diamond) is actually zirconium oxide. It is used in a lot of jewelry because it resembles a diamond but is much cheaper.

Zirconium is as useful as it is pretty. Zirconium oxide is also great for making heat-resistant and ultra-strong materials. A crucible (small bowl) made from ZrO_2 can be used to melt metals, and it does not crack even if placed into cold water after being heated. The nuclear power industry uses zirconium metal to line the inside of reactors and pipes, since it is not reactive with radioactive isotopes. This characteristic also makes it useful for implants in the human body, and it has been used for hip-replacement joints.

 Discovery Zone We have known about zirconium in gemstones since prehistoric times, but the pure element was very difficult to separate out of these compounds. Several scientists worked with zirconium compounds between 1789 and 1824 but were not able to purify the element. Much later, in 1924, chemists Anton Eduard van Arkel and Jan Hendrik de Boer extracted the pure metal from zirconium (II) chloride.

ELEMENTAL STATS

P+ 40
E- 40
N 51

State: Solid

Atomic Mass: 91.22 amu

Density: 6.52 g/cm³

Atomic Radius: 223 pm

Element Group: Transition Metals

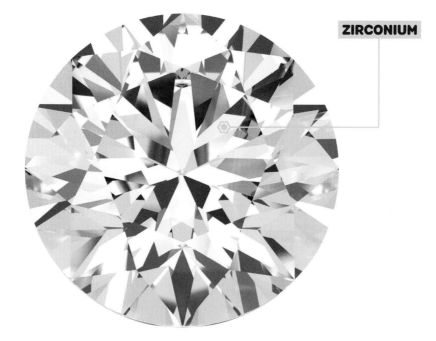

ZIRCONIUM

ELEMENTAL STATS

P+ 41
E- 41
N 52

State: Solid

Atomic Mass:
92.91 amu

Density:
8.57 g/cm³

Atomic Radius:
218 pm

Element Group:
Transition Metals

NIOBIUM

Niobium is always found with tantalum (#73) in nature as the mineral columbite. Once isolated, niobium is a very strong metal that reacts with the oxygen (#8) in the air.

Niobium serves as a very important element for transportation. It is used in making propeller blades for airplanes because it is a very stable metal. Niobium is also mixed with other metals to make alloys. Rockets and jet engines use stainless steel mixed with niobium to make the metal alloy even stronger. Another interesting use of niobium is for superconductive wire. These wires can conduct electricity better than other kinds of wires in use today; they are often found in high-tech medical and scientific equipment. They are also used at the Thomas Jefferson National Accelerator Facility, where scientists are studying matter even smaller than protons and neutrons.

Discovery Zone Niobium was initially called columbium, named in honor of Columbus, who at that time was credited with the discovery of America, where the element was first found. It was identified in 1801 by Charles Hatchett, from the mineral columbite. In the United States, the element was called columbium until the 1950s, when it was officially named niobium by the International Union of Pure and Applied Chemistry (IUPAC). And yes, there is an organization that controls the names of all chemicals!

NIOBIUM

MOLYBDENUM

42
Mo

ELEMENTAL STATS

P+ 42
E- 42
N 54

State: Solid
Atomic Mass: 95.95 amu
Density: 10.2 g/cm³
Atomic Radius: 217 pm
Element Group: Transition Metals

Most molybdenum is not used by itself, but rather in an alloy with other metals, such as nickel (#28) or steel. As is usual, the metal alloys are stronger, harder, and better electrical conductors. The molybdenum alloys end up in engines and tools such as drills and saw blades.

The most important use of molybdenum is in nature. About 50 different enzymes use molybdenum, and among these, the most important enzyme is nitrogenase. As the name implies, nitrogenase works on nitrogen (#7), breaking it apart and making it usable for plants and animals. The enzyme is found in bacteria that live on the roots of plants like peas, chickpeas, and peanuts. To work correctly, nitrogenase needs molybdenum, but it also uses the elements carbon (#6), iron (#26), and vanadium (#23).

Discovery Zone Carl Wilhelm Scheele is given the credit for discovering molybdenum. Isaac Asimov, a famous science fiction writer and scientist, referred to Scheele as "hard luck Scheele" because while he made a number of discoveries, most of the credit went elsewhere. The discovery of oxygen (#8) is most often credited to Antoine Lavoisier, while Scheele discovered it at least four years earlier. Part of the problem is that Scheele didn't always have the best equipment handy. While Scheele discovered molybdenum, he didn't prepare the pure metal first.

MOLYBDENUM

TECHNETIUM

State: Solid

Atomic Mass:
98 amu

Density:
11.5 g/cm³

Atomic Radius:
216 pm

Element Group:
Transition Metals

Technetium was the first man-made element. Based on the periodic table, chemists know there had to be an element #43, but no one could find it in nature. In fact, by 1925, there were only five "missing" elements on Mendeleev's table. After much effort and many incorrect claims, scientists were able to make #43 (not discover it).

Technetium's name comes from the Greek word for artificial, or "made by humans." No form of technetium stays around for too long. The atoms are all radioactive, meaning that the nucleus breaks apart by itself. Yet we can put the element's tendency to fall apart to good use.

Technetium is used a lot by pharmacists and doctors in healthcare treatments, helping cure some sick patients. While it is radioactive and must be handled carefully, it is *not dangerously* radioactive. Technetium medicines are safely used millions of times each year to treat patients.

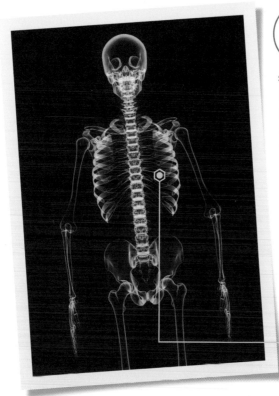

Discovery Zone
The search for technetium was a struggle. Some scientists thought they had discovered it in 1925 and named it masurium. Because no other scientist was able to repeat their experiment, the "discovery" was not accepted by the scientific world. It took 10 more years of effort before technetium was truly created by Emilio Segrè and Carlo Perrier in Italy in 1937.

TECHNETIUM

RUTHENIUM

44

Ru

Ruthenium is one of the rarest metals on Earth, so you will not find it in a lot of materials we use every day. It does make platinum (#78) and palladium (#46) harder when mixed as an alloy with these metals.

Ruthenium metal is useful in electronics and is a good conductor. Ruthenium compounds have also been used in solar cells, turning sunlight into electrical energy we can use to power our homes. Ruthenium catalysts are important in the production of plastics and other **polymers**, or large molecules made up of many similar smaller ones.

Discovery Zone Science experiments must be able to be replicated by others to be valid. Polish chemist Jędrzej Śniadecki first claimed to have discovered a new element in 1807. However, others could not repeat his experiment, so he canceled his claim and lost the naming privileges. The element was rediscovered in 1844 by Karl Karlovich Klaus, a Russian. It was named ruthenium, from the Latin word for Russia.

ELEMENTAL STATS

P+ 44
E- 44
N 57

State: Solid

Atomic Mass: 101.07 amu

Density: 12.1 g/cm³

Atomic Radius: 213 pm

Element Group: Transition Metals

RUTHENIUM

ELEMENTAL STATS

P+ 45
E- 45
N 58

State: Solid

Atomic Mass:
102.91 amu

Density:
12.4 g/cm³

Atomic Radius:
210 pm

Element Group:
Transition
Metals

RHODIUM

Rhodium is one of the rarest metals, so we don't have a lot of it, which makes it one of the most expensive metals as well. But rhodium is such a good catalyst that it is used in the chemical industry to speed up chemical reactions. Adding rhodium to platinum (#78) or palladium (#46) improves the heat resistance and endurance of the combined metals. You may have some rhodium alloys in the spark plugs of your family car.

Rhodium is also used as a catalyst in catalytic converters. Catalytic converters are very important for cleaning up car exhaust; the metal catalysts convert harmful gases released by the engine into less harmful gases. Actually, 80% of the rhodium we use goes into the production of catalytic converters.

Discovery Zone Rhodium is often found with platinum and palladium. Actually, the first rhodium sample came from trying to purify a platinum ore sample in 1803. William Hyde Wollaston was working on platinum ore and found multiple metals inside. He got several of the metals to dissolve in acids, but rhodium would not, and he was left with a red powder: a rhodium compound.

RHODIUM

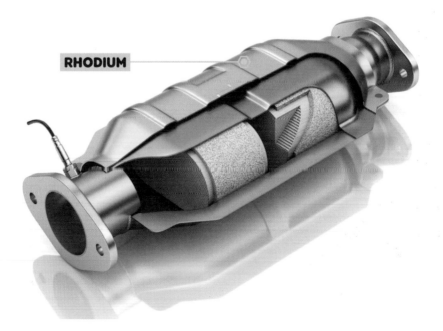

PALLADIUM

Palladium is part of the "platinum group" of metals, including ruthenium (#44), rhodium (#45), palladium, osmium (#76), iridium (#77), and platinum (#78). These metals have similar properties and can often be found in the same areas. They don't tarnish easily, which makes them good for jewelry. They are not very commonly found, with only one palladium mine in the United States. For this reason, palladium is expensive, too.

Palladium is found in electronic **capacitors**, simple electronic components that are used in devices like cell phones. Capacitors play different roles in cell phones, but they generally help prevent spikes in electric current.

Palladium is also used in an important component of your car's catalytic converter: Small amounts of palladium, rhodium, and platinum in the device increase the speed of chemical reactions, including changing the very poisonous carbon monoxide to the less dangerous carbon dioxide. It also converts toxic nitrogen oxide molecules back to pure oxygen (#8) and nitrogen (#7), the normal major parts of the air you breathe.

Before catalytic converters came standard in cars, big cities with lots of traffic were much more polluted than they are now. If you live in a city, you can thank palladium and catalytic converters for the reduced smog compared to 40 years ago.

 Discovery Zone William Hyde Wollaston discovered palladium in 1802, but did not immediately share the news—a somewhat risky ploy. What if someone else discovered the element and grabbed its naming rights? He anonymously provided some mineral to sell, claiming it was a new element. That created some buzz. Then, he presented the evidence for the new element at a scientific presentation in 1805!

ELEMENTAL STATS

P+ 46
E- 46
N 60

State: Solid
Atomic Mass: 106.42 amu
Density: 12.0 g/cm³
Atomic Radius: 210 pm
Element Group: Transition Metals

 PALLADIUM

ELEMENTAL STATS

P+ 47
E- 47
N 61

State: Solid

Atomic Mass:
107.87 amu

Density:
10.5 g/cm³

Atomic Radius:
211 pm

Element Group:
Transition Metals

SILVER

Have you noticed that some of the element symbols seem to make more sense than others? For instance, C for carbon (#6) seems logical, while Ag for silver may not—unless you know Latin, that is! *Argentum* is the Latin word for silver, leading to the symbol *Ag*.

Many people think of jewelry when hearing about silver, but pure silver is not tough enough to be used in jewelry. To overcome this problem, chemists have alloyed silver with other elements, like copper (#29). Sterling silver is 92.5% silver and 7.5% copper. It is still shiny and does not easily tarnish, so not only is it commonly used in jewelry, but also in silverware.

Silver is one of the best reflectors of light, making it useful as a mirror. Maybe more important is how compounds of silver change when exposed to light, making silver the original basis of photography. Even today, silver compounds are used to make the highest quality prints of digital photos.

Discovery Zone Humankind has treasured silver for thousands of years. In Turkey and Greece, archeologists have found evidence of silver mining dating back to 3000 BCE. On a sad note, the discovery of lots of silver in the New World by the Spanish conquistadors led to the takeover of the indigenous civilizations. For hundreds of years, 85% of the world's silver came from the conquered New World (present-day Bolivia, Peru, and Mexico).

SILVER

CADMIUM

Most people love to use their phones and portable devices, but don't often think about the batteries that make them possible. Cadmium combined with nickel (#28) is used to make the Ni/Cd rechargeable battery, which is used all over the world to power devices. In fact, more than 80% of the cadmium mined is used to make batteries for computers. One problem we have run into with cadmium is its toxicity. Cadmium is being phased out of many uses to decrease the potential for pollution.

Because cadmium is unreactive, it is used to coat stainless steel on bridges and airplanes to prevent corrosion (breakdown of the metal). Paints containing the metal cadmium often have a distinct yellow color. Cadmium is also used in nuclear power plants to absorb neutrons from the nuclear reaction. The cadmium-containing control rods can be inserted into the reaction chamber to slow down the rate at which uranium (#92) and plutonium (#94) undergo **nuclear fission**, or nucleus division.

 Discovery Zone Cadmium was discovered by Friedrich Stromeyer in 1817 as he tracked down the impurity in a zinc (#30) ore named calamine. The government asked him to start an investigation because some of the skin medicines in central Germany were discolored, and government leaders wanted to know why. He was able to collect the new element, naming it cadmium due to its presence in the calamine ore. It is always good to ask questions like "why" because they often lead to new discoveries.

ELEMENTAL STATS

P+ 48
E- 48
N 64

State: Solid

Atomic Mass: 112.41 amu

Density: 8.69 g/cm³

Atomic Radius: 218 pm

Element Group: Transition Metals

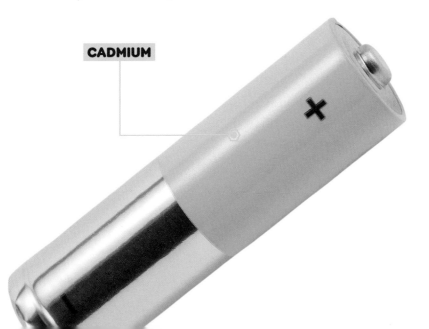

CADMIUM

INDIUM

State: Solid

Atomic Mass:
114.82 amu

Density:
7.31 g/cm³

Atomic Radius:
193 pm

Element Group:
Boron Family

ndium is a pretty rare metal, the 61st most abundant element in Earth's crust. Despite that, it is still three times more abundant than silver (#47). You may have never heard of indium, but we know you have used it. A compound of indium, indium tin oxide (ITO), is in every touch screen and flat screen you have used. So, every time you touch a cell phone or tablet, you're touching indium.

Why is it everywhere? Because ITO is transparent yet still conducts electricity very well. For this reason, it is also used in coating and protecting solar panels. Even welding masks use ITO as a coating. So, our modern world relies heavily on an element that almost no one thinks about. It has a few other cool uses—for example, as a lubricant in race cars—and was used in World War II for airplane engines.

Discovery Zone You have probably heard that it is important to be a "team player." This is true on the sports field and in the chemistry lab. While studying a mineral sample, Ferdinand Reich observed new lines with a spectroscope, suggesting a new element. But being color blind, he asked a colleague to check it out. Sure enough, Hieronymous Richter saw a new purple line. From this, they named the new element after its violet color. Unfortunately, the story does not end there. Apparently, Richter went off to conferences to take all the credit for the discovery, leading to the end of a friendship.

INDIUM

TIN

Did you know that tin cans are not made of tin? Oh, they are coated with tin, but the "tin can" is made up of mostly steel. The tin coating is important because it resists rust (also called corrosion). Once the tin can was invented, food could be sealed and stored for months.

If you look in your pantry, chances are there are some canned food items. They are handy because the food lasts a long time, and the cans do not corrode. While most cans used for food are aluminum (#13) now, they used to be made of tin.

Tin is also responsible for the Bronze Age (around 3000 BCE–1200 BCE). Most tin today is used in alloys such as bronze or pewter, but it was during this era when humans first began using tin with copper (#29) to make bronze. Bronze is made when a little tin is added to copper, making for tougher and stronger tools and allowing humans to complete more difficult tasks.

 Discovery Zone As mentioned earlier, tin played an important role in human civilization. It has been used all around the world. Archeologists have found evidence of the use of tin across many cultures, from Egypt to China to the Incas in Peru. We don't know who first collected tin, but we do know that a lot of people have seen it as a useful element for a very long time.

ELEMENTAL STATS

P+ 50
E- 50
N 69

State: Solid

Atomic Mass: 118.71 amu

Density: 7.29 g/cm³

Atomic Radius: 217 pm

Element Group: Carbon Family

TIN

ANTIMONY

State: Solid

Atomic Mass:
121.76 amu

Density:
6.68 g/cm³

Atomic Radius:
206 pm

Element Group:
Pnictogens

Semiconductors are everywhere. They are in our phones, televisions, and everyday electronic devices. Antimony is one of the metals used to make semiconductors. It is also used in making diodes, a component of LED lights. LEDs are becoming the first choice for lighting because they use much less energy than other light sources, and using less energy helps save the planet.

Antimony can be alloyed with other metals and with glass to improve their hardness. Another place you will find antimony is alloyed with lead (#82) in bullets. Forensic chemists use the amount of antimony to tell the difference between different kinds of bullets. Through such chemical analysis, we can help make sure that the correct people are going to jail for crimes involving guns.

 Discovery Zone Antimony has been around since prehistoric times. Our students always ask, "Why is the symbol for antimony Sb?" It comes from antimony's first name, "stibium," a reference to the ore stibnite, from which it was first collected. Nicolas Lémery was the person who made antimony "famous" by studying it and publishing his findings in 1707.

ANTIMONY

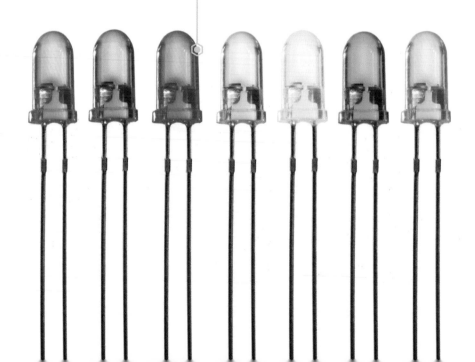

TELLURIUM

52
Te

Tellurium is an interesting element for an odd reason. There are almost no biological uses for it and only a few commercial ones. But humans are creative and have found that when combined with another dangerous element, cadmium (#48), it forms telluride, which can be used as a semiconductor for computers and solar panels. The CdTe material may even have one of the smallest carbon footprints, and makes the most energy for each solar panel. However, some people are still fearful about its use, since both cadmium and tellurium are toxic by themselves.

Solar panels are not our first use of tellurium, though. For a while, DVDs were the most high-tech way to store data. DVDs used a coating made from a tellurium and oxygen (#8) compound. While DVDs were certainly an upgrade from watching movies on videotape, technology continues to evolve. Have you used your DVD player lately? As technology changes, the world of chemistry moves along with it.

 Discovery Zone When you hear the name *Transylvania*, do you think of Count Dracula? That is supposedly where Dracula came from. But did you know the element tellurium was first found there, too? Franz-Joseph Müller von Reichenstein studied an ore for several years, finally deciding that it was a new element. But did he tell the world? Well, sort of. He published his findings in a journal not read by many chemists, so not many people heard about his discovery. Fortunately for Müller, Martin Heinrich Klaproth became interested in Müller's findings and confirmed the new element 15 years later.

ELEMENTAL STATS

P+ 52
E- 52
N 76

State: Solid

Atomic Mass: 127.6 amu

Density: 6.23 g/cm³

Atomic Radius: 206 pm

Element Group: Chalcogens

TELLURIUM

IODINE

State: Solid

Atomic Mass:
126.9 amu

Density:
4.93 g/cm³

Atomic Radius:
198 pm

Element Group:
Halogens

We need iodine in its ion form, I⁻, every day to be healthy. The thyroid gland in our bodies uses iodide (I⁻) to help regulate our body temperature and growth. Fortunately, we do not need to worry about getting iodine because our food contains plenty of it. For example, table salt has added iodide to make sure we are getting plenty of it in our diets.

Take a look at your table salt container. If it is "iodized salt," it contains sodium chloride (NaCl) and sodium iodide (NaI). Iodide and chloride are the ions of iodine and chlorine (#17). Like many of the halogens, iodine is found in seawater as the iodide ion. Many cultures use seaweed in their diets. Keep eating your seaweed, as pure iodine is toxic and more reactive than the iodide ion.

Iodine also has uses beyond our bodies. It is used in photographic film in the form of potassium iodide and as an antimicrobial in iodine solution.

Discovery Zone Iodine was accidently discovered by Bernard Courtois in 1811 while he was working in his family's saltpeter (potassium nitrate) business. Saltpeter is an important component of gunpowder, fertilizers, and food preservatives. Courtois added extra acid to some seaweed in his experiment and noticed a purple gas that started forming a solid when it touched cooler surfaces in his lab. The purple-black solid was pure iodine.

IODINE

XENON

Xenon is at the end of a row on the periodic table, in a column with other noble gases. Noble gases are not chemically reactive, as they have all the electrons they need. This means that chemists have a difficult time making compounds with them. However, way back in 1962, chemist Neil Bartlett was able to get xenon to react with the most reactive element on the periodic table, fluorine (#9). Since that time, chemists have been able to make about 100 xenon compounds. That may sound like a lot, but consider that there are more than one million carbon compounds.

Scientists have put xenon to use as a **propellant** in ion propulsion engines, along with rubidium (#37) and cesium (#55). Xenon is actually the most common material used for ion propulsion engines. There are satellites flying over our heads right now using xenon.

If that isn't enough, have you heard of dark matter? It is a mysterious material we don't know much about, yet it may hold the key to understanding the universe. Scientists are using xenon to search for dark matter because it's not too reactive, and it has a large enough nucleus to collide with dark matter.

ELEMENTAL STATS

P+ 54
E- 54
N 77

State: Gas

Atomic Mass: 131.29 amu

Density: 0.00537 g/cm³

Atomic Radius: 216 pm

Element Group: Noble Gases

Discovery Zone

Two chemists, William Ramsay and Morris Travers, discovered xenon in 1898. We have already learned about them because they also discovered neon (#10), argon (#18), and krypton (#36). They were able to discover so many noble gases because they accepted the challenge put forth by Lord Rayleigh in 1894. Lord Rayleigh was not sure why the density of nitrogen (#7) changed depending on how it was collected. This odd observation led to the discovery of all the noble gases.

XENON

CESIUM

State: Solid

Atomic Mass:
132.91 amu

Density:
1.87 g/cm³

Atomic Radius:
343 pm

Element Group:
Alkali Metals

Have you ever heard of an atomic clock? Atomic clocks are used by satellite and phone networks to make sure everyone is on the same, accurate time. Cesium is used in atomic clocks to produce time that is accurate to within one second in 15 million years. You have no excuses for being late to school if you are using a cesium clock! Recently, NASA released an announcement about a deep-space atomic clock made from mercury (#80) ions, which is even better than the cesium-based clock (see mercury, page 99), so cesium has some competition.

Metallic cesium is very reactive, like all the alkali metals. Actually, the reactivity of the alkali metals increases as you go down the periodic table. Cesium, which is close to the bottom, can't be exposed to moisture in air or any form of water. The metal will react immediately, producing cesium hydroxide, CsOH, and hydrogen gas, H_2. Cesium hydroxide is one of the strongest bases known and will even react with glass.

Once cesium is in a compound, it is safer to work with and is used in photoelectric cells (solar panels) and as a catalyst to make sulfuric acid. Cesium ions, like rubidium (#37) ions, are used by NASA in engines for spacecraft.

Discovery Zone In 1860, Robert Bunsen and Gustav Kirchhoff were studying mineral water and noticed an interesting blue color in the spectral lines emitted from the elements in the water. The scientists named cesium based on its blue color, using the Latin word for "sky blue": *caesius*.

CESIUM

BARIUM

Barium is very reactive and is never found as a pure metal in nature. It immediately reacts with oxygen (#8) in the air and water vapor. However, we run into barium most often as barium sulfate, $BaSO_4$ and barium carbonate, $BaCO_3$.

Barium sulfate helps medical professionals get good x-rays of your stomach and intestines. In these cases, you are handed a chalky mixture of the barium sulfate to drink before the x-ray. As the substance passes through your body, an x-ray picture is taken and doctors can see your soft tissue (muscles) because the $BaSO_4$ blocks the x-ray, and the tissues appear more clearly in the images.

Barium sulfate is also used as a filler in rubber and plastic to take up space, giving a larger volume of material. This is common in toys and car tires. Meanwhile, barium carbonate is used in bricks and cement. A slightly more exciting use of barium compounds is in fireworks. These compounds produce a beautiful green light when exploded during celebrations.

ELEMENTAL STATS

P+ 56
E- 56
N 81

State: Solid

Atomic Mass: 137.33 amu

Density: 3.62 g/cm³

Atomic Radius: 268 pm

Element Group: Alkaline Earth Metals

Discovery Zone

Because barium reacts with oxygen immediately, it makes sense that it was first discovered as barium oxide (BaO). In 1808, Sir Humphry Davy purified the metal by running electricity through BaO (adding electrons). This made the barium ions (Ba^{2+}) gain electrons and reduce to the pure metal.

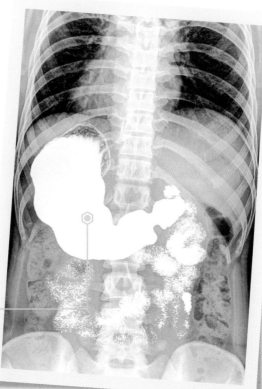

BARIUM

State: Solid

Atomic Mass:
138.91 amu

Density:
6.15 g/cm³

Atomic Radius:
243 pm

Element Group:
Lanthanides

LANTHANUM

As we enter the lanthanide elements, starting with lanthanum itself, we will find that these metals are either not used very much or they have very specialized uses. If you have ever gone camping, you may have seen a gas-mantle lantern. These lanterns use a mesh of metal oxides, including lanthanum, that increase their light's brightness.

More recently, lanthanum has found use in batteries. The lanthanum helps with movement of electrons through the battery, allowing them to charge faster and last longer. It was used for many years in nickel metal hydride (NMH) rechargeable batteries in hybrid vehicles such as the Toyota Prius. Recently, though, car manufacturers have started to favor lithium (#3) ion batteries. Each NMH battery needed more than 20 pounds of lanthanum!

Discovery Zone

We have already seen that Jöns Jacob Berzelius discovered silicon (#14) and selenium (#34). However, he influenced even more element discoveries by training chemists. One of his students, Carl Gustaf Mosander, discovered lanthanum, but it was Berzelius who suggested the name *lanthana*, meaning "to lie hidden." He made his discovery in 1839, but it took chemists until 1923 to prepare a pure form of the metal.

LANTHANUM

CERIUM

erium is the most abundant rare earth element. There is actually more cerium in Earth's crust than tin (#50) or lead (#82) and just about as much as zinc (#30). So, while it is called a rare earth metal, it is not very rare.

Cerium is found in nature in different ores, but is used mainly in alloys with other metals. One such alloy is known as mischmetal. It is used in lighters because cerium makes sparks when struck. Check with your family to see if you have a self-cleaning oven. If so, you use cerium (III) oxide to help keep your oven clean. It is coated onto the inside of self-cleaning ovens to speed up the breakdown of oils splattered inside, making them easier to clean. Meanwhile, cerium sulfide has a brilliant red color and is used in paints.

Discovery Zone Since Wilhelm Hisinger and Jöns Jacob Berzelius, as well as Martin Klaproth (working in a different laboratory), discovered the element in the same year, they all end up sharing credit. Hisinger and Berzelius published their data first, but Klaproth actually had the pure cerium first.

ELEMENTAL STATS

P+ 58
E- 58
N 82

State: Solid

Atomic Mass: 140.11 amu

Density: 6.77 g/cm³

Atomic Radius: 242 pm

Element Group: Lanthanides

CERIUM

ELEMENTAL STATS

P+ 59
E- 59
N 82

State: Solid

Atomic Mass:
144.91 amu

Density:
6.77 g/cm³

Atomic Radius:
240 pm

Element Group:
Lanthanides

PRASEODYMIUM

The word praseodymium comes from the Greek words *prasios* and *didymos*, meaning "green twin," because it resembles neodymium (#60), which was discovered at the same time. Scientists collect praseodymium from monazite sand, a difficult task, making it tricky for chemists to find the element initially.

As an alloy, it is used in aircraft engines and magnets. Praseodymium compounds also provide a good yellow coloring for ceramic glazes. It also makes up a small percentage of mischmetal, the stuff used in lighters and flints. The lights used in the movie industry, called carbon arc lights, also contain praseodymium.

Fiber-optic cables, which help us access the internet, also contain praseodymium, as do some safety goggles used by welders and glass blowers. In fact, it's the praseodymium that gives these goggles their yellowish color.

Discovery Zone Carl Mosander, the discoverer of lanthanum (#57), terbium (#65), and erbium (#68), caused some confusion by announcing a new element, didymium. For more than 40 years, didymium was listed as an element. In 1885, everything changed when Carl Auer von Welsbach showed that didymium was a mixture. Hidden inside the mixture were new elements, praseodymium and neodymium.

PRASEODYMIUM

NEODYMIUM

Have you ever used a small laser pointer to play with your cat? Cats love to chase the red or green dots around the floor. Neodymium is one of the elements used to make these pointers. Higher energy neodymium lasers are also used for the treatment of skin cancers and even in eye surgery.

Special glass is also made with neodymium mixed in. Glasses made with neodymium protect welders' and glass blowers' eyes from the very bright light produced in their work. Neodymium is very important for making electronic devices smaller because it is part of the alloy used to make very strong magnets. A small neodymium magnet (neodymium alloyed with iron [#26] and boron [#5]) can replace a large magnet yet have the same strength.

 Discovery Zone Sometimes, a mistake leads to other good things, like didymium. Chemist Carl Mosander made a mistake in calling didymium an element. Unfortunately, other chemists did not know this and Di was placed on the periodic table until Carl Auer von Welsbach separated neodymium and praseodymium (#59) from didymium in 1885. Out of one "element," we actually got two!

ELEMENTAL STATS

P+ 60
E- 60
N 84

State: Solid

Atomic Mass: 144.24 amu

Density: 7.01 g/cm³

Atomic Radius: 239 pm

Element Group: Lanthanides

NEODYMIUM

61
Pm

P+ 61
E- 61
N 84

State: Solid

Atomic Mass:
145 amu

Density:
7.26 g/cm³

Atomic Radius:
238 pm

Element Group:
Lanthanides

PROMETHIUM

Promethium is named after named after Prometheus, a Titan from Greek mythology. Prometheus is a champion of humankind for stealing fire from the gods to give to us. Maybe the element was named after Prometheus because it glows (like fire)?

Promethium is a rare earth element, and it is the only radioactive one in this group. It does not have many uses, but it has been used in batteries for pacemakers, which can stabilize a person's heart.

 Discovery Zone As you look at the periodic table now, it appears complete, with one element after the next. However, this was not always the case. Promethium is between neodymium (#60) and samarium (#62). But neodymium and samarium were discovered first. The "missing" element created an element hunt about 100 years ago. Many chemists thought they had discovered it. But the true discoverers, Jacob A. Marinsky, Lawrence E. Glendenin, and Charles D. Coryell, got to name it, and they chose promethium.

62
Sm

P+ 62
E- 62
N 88

State: Solid

Atomic Mass:
150.36 amu

Density:
7.52 g/cm³

Atomic Radius:
242 pm

Element Group:
Lanthanides

SAMARIUM

An isotope of samarium is used in an anti-cancer treatment medicine. Samarium can be used for studio lighting and projecting bright light as well.

Samarium was the first element to be named for a person. In this case, chemists detected the new element in a mineral called samarskite. Samarskite was named after a Russian colonel, Vassili Samarsky-Bykhovets. Does it seem fair to all the hardworking chemists that the person whose name was used had nothing to do with discovering elements? Well, think about this: We discovered many elements by looking at minerals from mines, and Colonel Samarsky was the Russian Chairman of the Board of Mining Engineers.

 Discovery Zone In 1853, Jean Charles Galissard de Marignac used light to detect samarium for the first time. After that, it took more than 25 years—until 1879—for samarium to be isolated by Paul-Émile Lecoq de Boisbaudran.

EUROPIUM

O f all of the lanthanides, europium is the most reactive, so it does not have many uses. Europe uses europium in its money production so that people cannot counterfeit their money. The added europium glows under a special ultra-violet light bulb, which allows people to check to see if the money is real. The europium oxide produces a red or blue glow, depending on the charge on the europium metal.

Europium oxide is also added to glowing materials, such as tele-visions and computer monitors. If europium (+3) oxide is used, the glow is red. If europium (+2) oxide is used, the glow is blue. When both europium oxides are combined in a light bulb, a white light is observed. This is the light you see in the new, low-energy light bulbs.

 Discovery Zone Remember the didymium we were talking about in the section on the element neodymium (#60)? That sample was not actually an element, but rather contained some (that is, multiple) undiscovered elements. Eugène-Anatole Demarçay was the first to catch on to this and was able to produce reasonably pure europium from the sample in 1901. Europium is named after Europe, as it was purified in France. It makes us wonder, why not name it francium? Ah, but the world had to wait until 1939 for that one!

ELEMENTAL STATS

P+ 63
E- 63
N 89

State: Solid

Atomic Mass: 151.96 amu

Density: 5.24 g/cm³

Atomic Radius: 235 pm

Element Group: Lanthanides

EUROPIUM

ELEMENTAL STATS

P+ 64
E- 64
N 93

State: Solid

Atomic Mass:
157.25 amu

Density:
7.90 g/cm³

Atomic Radius:
234 pm

Element Group:
Lanthanides

GADOLINIUM

Have you ever heard of MRI or magnetic resonance imaging? MRI machines are used by healthcare professionals to look at the inside of patients, like with an x-ray, but better! To get really good pictures of a patient's insides, they are given a gadolinium compound. The compound highlights the unhealthy tissues much differently than the healthy ones, allowing doctors to make the correct diagnosis.

Gadolinium is also used in nuclear power plants because this element grabs neutrons. Nuclear power plants rely on controlling the flow of neutrons to control the amount of nuclear fission. Power plants are really effective at making energy we can use to power our homes, but they also use very dangerous elements. In this case, gadolinium makes these plants safer.

Discovery Zone Way back when we introduced you to yttrium (#39), do you remember we ran across the name Johan Gadolin? Because of Gadolin's earlier discovery, Jean Charles Galissard de Marignac decided to honor Johan by naming a new element after him in 1880, so we now have gadolinium. And gadolinium is much more useful than yttrium. So, is it better to have discovered a somewhat useful element, or to have a really useful element named after you?

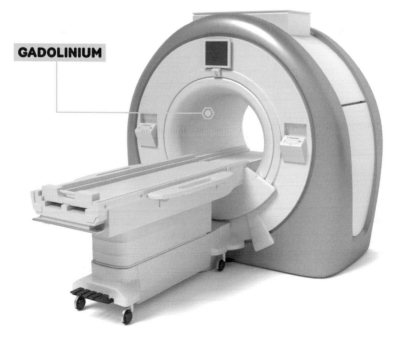

GADOLINIUM

TERBIUM

Terbium does not have a use as a pure metal, but in compounds and alloys, terbium has become very useful. Sodium terbium borate is used in semiconductors and is placed into fuel cells (which produce electricity) to help them withstand very high temperatures.

Under ultraviolet light, terbium glows green; it is placed into Euro notes (money), like europium (#63), to prevent counterfeiting. It is also used as an alloy with dysprosium (#66) and iron (#26) to make a small device that can turn any flat surface into a powerful speaker. Some stores have attached them to their front windows, turning their storefronts into loudspeakers. While regular speakers push air, terbium pushes solids, which is why terbium speakers work when attached to a store window or other flat surface.

Discovery Zone In 1843, Carl Gustaf Mosander was working on the ore gadolinite, a material containing a bunch of different elements, when he hit the element jackpot by isolating yttrium (#39) and two other new elements. In honor of Ytterby, the town in Sweden where the ores were discovered, he called these erbium (#68) and terbium.

ELEMENTAL STATS

P+ 65
E- 65
N 94

State: Solid

Atomic Mass:
158.93 amu

Density:
8.23 g/cm^3

Atomic Radius:
233 pm

Element Group:
Lanthanides

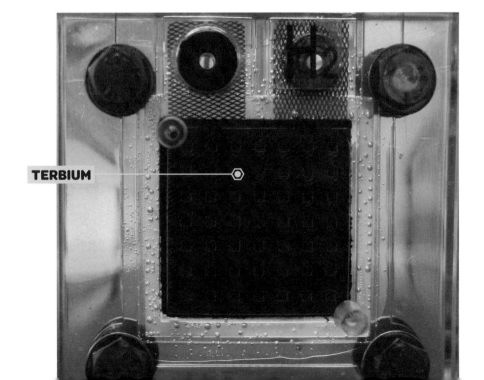

TERBIUM

66
Dy

ELEMENTAL STATS

P+ 66
E- 66
N 97

State: Solid

Atomic Mass:
162.5 amu

Density:
8.25 g/cm³

Atomic Radius:
231 pm

Element Group:
Lanthanides

DYSPROSIUM

Dysprosium, like the other lanthanides, is difficult to separate from the complex mixture in which it is found. The lanthanides are often found together, and many people have tried to separate them. Dysprosium was not purified until 1950, which is pretty recent, as far as the elements go.

As a pure metal, it is very reactive and reacts with air and water. Neodymium (#60) magnets actually contain some dysprosium as an alloy. The alloy makes the magnet stronger and allows it to work at higher temperatures. We need magnets to work at high temperatures because they are used in motors, which heat up while in use. Higher-temperature magnets are also used in wind turbines and electric cars. Such clean energy allows us to use less fossil fuels, like gasoline and coal, which are harmful to the environment.

Discovery Zone In 1886, Paul-Émile Lecoq de Boisbaudran discovered dysprosium in a sample of yttrium oxide. Scientists studied the yttrium oxide sample from 1794 for many years and kept finding new elements in it. Several lanthanides were discovered from this sample. Erbium (#68) was found in 1843, holmium (#67) in 1878, and finally dysprosium in 1886.

DYSPROSIUM

HOLMIUM

As far as we can tell, holmium and its compounds have no commercial use. Maybe someone like you will find a good use for it because holmium has a high magnetic permeability, which means you may be able to make data storage devices out of holmium that won't be damaged by a magnet.

Per Teodor Cleve, who first isolated holmium, had an even greater scientific effect by training great chemists. He trained the first woman to earn her doctorate degree in Sweden—Ellen Fries. Cleve also trained Svante Arrhenius (above), who won the Nobel Prize in Chemistry in 1903 and is one of the most important chemists in history. In addition to helping women advance in the sciences, Cleve developed ion concepts that we use every day in chemistry. He was so far ahead of his time that he even predicted that carbon dioxide would cause global climate change!

 Discovery Zone In 1878, Swiss chemists Marc Delafontaine and Jacques-Louis Soret observed a possible new element but could do no better than noting that "element X" had been discovered. At almost the same time, Swedish chemist Per Teodor Cleve isolated holmium while studying the ore erbia, not to be confused with erbium (#68). We will see Per Teodor Cleve again because erbia contained not just this new element but also thulium (#69).

ELEMENTAL STATS

P+ 67
E- 67
N 98

State: Solid

Atomic Mass: 164.93 amu

Density: 8.8 g/cm³

Atomic Radius: 230 pm

Element Group: Lanthanides

68

Er

ELEMENTAL STATS

P+ 68
E- 68
N 99

State: Solid

Atomic Mass:
167.26 amu

Density:
9.07 g/cm³

Atomic Radius:
229 pm

Element Group:
Lanthanides

ERBIUM

Even though it appears toward the end of the lanthanides, erbium was one of the first elements in the row to be discovered. Sadly, erbium has only a few uses, mostly as an additive to other materials. For example, when erbium is added to fiber-optic glass, it helps improve the signal, making high-definition television a reality. Adding erbium to glass gives it a pink coloring. It is also used in welding goggles to protect the workers' eyes.

Erbium, like yttrium (#39), ytterbium (#70), and terbium (#65), is named after the town in Sweden where it was discovered. From one ore—gadolinite—several new elements were discovered! But between different chemists studying the new elements and erbium and terbium having very similar properties, some confusion ensued. A name swap occurred, so what was originally called erbium is now called terbium, and the original terbium is now erbium. Note-keeping and good communication are important to science!

Discovery Zone We learned about erbium while learning about terbium. If you remember, Carl Mosander was studying ores from Ytterby, Sweden, when he discovered both elements. While erbium was identified in the ore and accepted as an element by the chemical community, it took 91 years for chemists to get pure erbium.

ERBIUM

THULIUM

State: olid
Atomic Mass:
168.93 amu
Density:
9.32 g/cm³
Atomic Radius:
227 pm
Element Group:
Lanthanides

Thule is the historic name for Scandinavia. Per Teodor Cleve, the discoverer of the element, chose the name *thulium* to honor his home region. As we get to the bottom of the periodic table, we are learning about some of the less known and less common elements.

Thulium is about as available as gold (#79) or silver (#47) and is used in money as protection from counterfeiting. If you shine a black light on thulium, it glows blue. The cost of thulium also keeps it from being commonly used, although some x-ray machines and surgical lasers contain small amounts of thulium.

 Discovery Zone Cleve discovered thulium in 1879 as he was re-examining erbium (#68). He noticed there were "leftovers" after cleaning up the erbium, and he guessed that the remaining material might be another new element. As it turned out, he was right.

YTTERBIUM

State: Solid
Atomic Mass:
173.05 amu
Density:
6.90 g/cm³
Atomic Radius:
226 pm
Element Group:
Lanthanides

Ytterbium is connected with yttrium (#39), terbium (#65), erbium (#68), and lutetium (#71). These elements all came from the same area of Ytterby, Sweden, which you have already read about (and will hear about one more time)!

While discovering ytterbium was challenging, we have not found much use for the element. Ytterbium is used in fiber-optic cables and can be added to stainless steel, but that's about it. Some scientists are studying it for use in computer memory chips, and some suggest it could be used as a catalyst in organic chemistry reactions.

 Discovery Zone Ytterbium was discovered by French chemist Jean Charles Galissard de Marignac in 1878. He was studying a sample of erbium when he discovered a hidden impurity, naming it ytterbium. However, the story does not end there. In 1907, another French chemist, Georges Urbain, found that the element ytterbium also had an impurity. Urbain found lutetium (#71).

LUTETIUM

State: Solid

Atomic Mass:
174.97 amu

Density:
9.84 g/cm³

Atomic Radius:
224 pm

Element Group:
Lanthanides

Lutetium is the last of the lanthanides. While there are not many different uses for lutetium, it does have an important use as a catalyst for **hydrocarbon cracking**, the breaking down of complex carbon molecules into smaller ones, an essential process in making fuel. So, we can thank lutetium for many of the fuels, like gasoline, that we use daily. The element is named for the Roman Empire's name for Paris, Lutetia, since credit for the discovery went to the French chemist Georges Urbain.

However, Charles James, working in the United States, provided a cleaner sample of the new element. James focused on providing clean (pure) samples of the rare earth elements, and he became an expert on purifying them. His process for purifying the rare earth elements was *the* method for almost 40 years, and it came to be called the James method.

 Discovery Zone Lutetium was not discovered until 1907, with credit going to both Georges Urbain from France and Charles James from the United States. James may not have discovered it first, but he worked hard to collect a pure sample of the new element. His extra efforts kept him from publishing his results until after Urbain.

LUTETIUM

HAFNIUM

Hafnium was the next-to-last element to be discovered in Earth's crust, partly due to its chemical behavior. It is in the same column as zirconium (#40). They are found together in nature, and it is very difficult to separate them.

The element is used a lot in the nuclear energy industry because it absorbs neutrons very well. Inside a nuclear energy plant, the amount of neutrons controls how much energy is produced. More neutrons yield more energy. Hafnium is used in the control rods. If you want more power, you pull the control rods out. If you want less power, you put the rods into the reactor core to absorb the neutrons and slow down the nuclear reaction.

ELEMENTAL STATS

P+ 72
E- 72
N 106

State: Solid

Atomic Mass: 178.49 amu

Density: 13.3 g/cm³

Atomic Radius: 223 pm

Element Group: Transition Metals

Discovery Zone

Hafnium remained a "missing" element for many years after Dmitri Mendeleev wrote out his periodic table. Georges Urbain claimed to have discovered it in 1911. However, Urbain's new element, celtium, acted as a lanthanide, not quite fitting into its spot on the periodic table, so eventually his claim was rejected. Finally, in 1923, George Charles de Hevesy and Dirk Coster were able to collect hafnium.

HAFNIUM

73

Ta

ELEMENTAL STATS

P+ 73
E- 73
N 108

State: Solid

Atomic Mass:
180.95 amu

Density:
16.4 g/cm³

Atomic Radius:
222 pm

Element Group:
Transition
Metals

TANTALUM

About half of all of the tantalum that is used ends up in the semiconductors of phones or computers. As most people want their communication electronics to be pocket-size, tantalum electronic parts are becoming more popular because they can be made especially small. Tantalum is also very hard and resistant to corroding, so it has been used in the high-tech worlds of rockets and jet engines.

Even cooler is tantalum's use in making replacement parts for the human body. You may even know someone with a hip replacement or new knee joint. Tantalum can make these modern medical achievements possible because most people's bodies accept this element, unlike other metals (which our bodies reject). Tantalum can be used to craft everything from new hips and knees to skull plates!

 Discovery Zone In 1802, Anders Ekeberg discovered tantalum in Sweden. If you look at the periodic table, you'll see that tantalum is right below niobium (#41), meaning it has similar chemical properties. The similarity led to a scientific dispute, as other scientists argued that Ekeberg had just collected an impure sample of niobium, not a distinct new element. It took another 44 years for scientists to agree that tantalum was an element—and another 57 years after that before Heinrich Rose made pure tantalum.

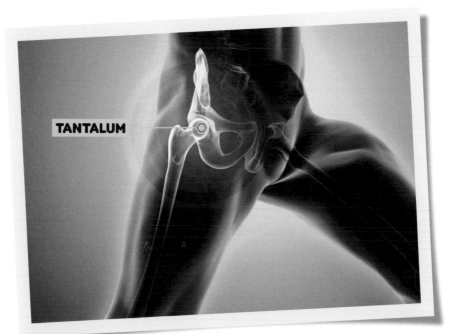

TANTALUM

TUNGSTEN

Tungsten does not melt until it is heated to over 6,000°F. Being tough to melt made tungsten the element to use in the old incandescent light bulbs. One of the reasons we have replaced the old light bulbs with LED bulbs is that incandescent light bulbs got so hot.

Because of its high melting point, tungsten gets used in welding and in the heating parts of many furnaces. Not only is tungsten heat-resistant, but it is also really hard. Scientists use the Mohs scale to compare hardness. A diamond has a Mohs value of 10, the hardest possible rating. Tungsten has a Mohs value of 7.5, but combine it with carbon (#6) to make tungsten carbide, and you get a Mohs value of 9, making it useful for drilling. So maybe your dentist has a new ultra-fast drill made of tungsten carbide!

ELEMENTAL STATS

P+ 74
E- 74
N 110

State: Solid

Atomic Mass: 183.84 amu

Density: 19.3 g/cm³

Atomic Radius: 218 pm

Element Group: Transition Metals

Discovery Zone People used tungsten for many years without ever collecting the pure element. Chinese crafters used a tungsten material that gave their pottery a peach color. But tungsten was not purified as an element until 1783. Chemist brothers Juan José and Fausto Elhuyar collected tungsten in Spain from the mineral wolframite, giving us the symbol W, for "wolfram."

TUNGSTEN

ELEMENTAL STATS

P+ 75
E- 75
N 111

State: Solid

Atomic Mass:
186.21 amu

Density:
20.8 g/cm³

Atomic Radius:
216 pm

Element Group:
Transition
Metals

RHENIUM

Rhenium does not have many industrial uses. As one of the rarest elements in Earth's crust, it is both expensive and somewhat difficult to get, though it's not as expensive as gold (#79), platinum (#78), or rhodium (#45).

Because it is so hard, rhenium can be used as an electrical connector. It was also used in flashes for photography. Rhenium and other elements are used as catalysts to speed up chemical reactions, such as hydrogenation, which we discussed in the section on nickel (#28).

Remember, after Dmitri Mendeleev introduced the periodic table, scientists liked that it predicted the chemistry of undiscovered elements. Mendeleev's table sparked scientific races to discover the predicted elements, but not all the races were fast. Rhenium was one of the tougher elements to discover even though chemists knew it would be a lot like manganese (#25).

Discovery Zone
Walter Noddack, Ida Tacke, and Otto Berg collected rhenium in 1925 from gadolinite, the mineral that also gave us cerium (#58), lanthanum (#57), neodymium (#60), and yttrium (#39). No wonder it was so hard to find!

RHENIUM

OSMIUM

Partly due to its expense, osmium is a rarely used element. Osmium is also pretty rare but is found in nickel (#28) ores. As nickel is purified, we get osmium as a side product, giving the mining companies two products from the same rocks. It is nice when you have more products to sell.

Alloys of osmium are so hard that they can be used as needles or tips for old-school fountain pens. The element can act as a catalyst to speed up chemical reactions and is sometimes used in industry for hydrogenation.

Discovery Zone As we have seen, it is important for scientists to examine all parts of an experiment. While studying platinum (#78) in 1803, Smithson Tennant noticed some non-platinum residue. While others may have ignored it, Tennant carefully studied it and found not just one new element but two—iridium (#77) and osmium!

ELEMENTAL STATS

P+ 76
E- 76
N 114

State: Solid

Atomic Mass: 190.23 amu

Density: 22.59 g/cm³

Atomic Radius: 216 pm

Element Group: Transition Metals

OSMIUM

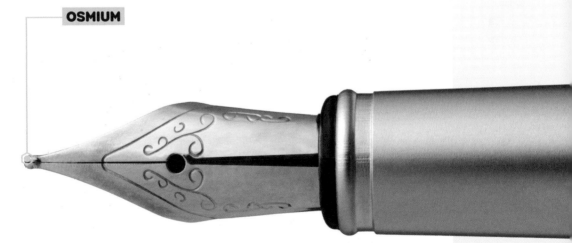

ELEMENTAL STATS

P+ 77
E- 77
N 115

State: Solid

Atomic Mass: 192.22 amu

Density: 22.56 g/cm³

Atomic Radius: 213 pm

Element Group: Transition Metals

IRIDIUM

Iridium was named for the Latin word for rainbow, *iris*, because iridium compounds display a lot of different colors. Iridium (III) chloride ($IrCl_3$) is green, while iridium tetrachloride ($IrCl_4$) can be purple. Meanwhile, iridium combined with oxygen (#8) creates a dark blue color.

Because the element is very hard but breaks easily, it is added to osmium (#76) to make old-school fountain pens. It also does not corrode (or react) easily, so it is used in spark plugs that must work in very tough conditions.

Scientists have found a buried, very thin layer of iridium around the whole world. The iridium layer provides evidence that meteors (which often contain lots of iridium) struck the planet, causing massive climate change and killing off many plants and animals. This was unfortunate for the dinosaurs, but it allowed mammals like us to take over.

Discovery Zone While studying platinum (#78), English chemist Smithson Tennant discovered two elements—osmium and iridium—in 1803. He was also responsible for confirming that diamond and charcoal are both carbon (#6).

IRIDIUM

PLATINUM

Platinum is a silvery metal that does not tarnish because it is not reactive in air. This kind of metal is called a noble metal. Platinum is commonly used in jewelry because it is not only pretty but very strong and rare. It is also quite expensive.

Platinum is one of the metals used for the important process of removing pollutants from our car exhaust. The catalytic converters in your parents' cars contain platinum as a catalyst, which helps carbon monoxide and nitrogen oxides react to form less toxic gases so they do not reach the air we breathe. Platinum is great for laboratory equipment as well because it is an unreactive metal. It has also been incorporated into some cool molecules like cisplatin, which is used to treat cancer.

Discovery Zone Ancient Egyptian and South American artifacts made of platinum and other precious metals, such as gold (#79) and silver (#47), date back thousands of years BCE. Antonio de Ulloa was credited with its discovery when he returned to Spain in 1746 with platinum samples and noted that the silver-looking metal had properties that differed from other known metals.

ELEMENTAL STATS

P+ 78
E- 78
N 117

State: Solid

Atomic Mass: 195.08 amu

Density: 21.5 g/cm³

Atomic Radius: 175 pm

Element Group: Transition Metals

PLATINUM

GOLD

ELEMENTAL STATS

P+ 79
E- 79
N 118

State: Solid

Atomic Mass:
196.97 amu

Density:
19.3 g/cm³

Atomic Radius:
214 pm

Element Group:
Transition
Metals

Gold is shiny and malleable, meaning that we can bang it into a bunch of different shapes. This, along with its beautiful color and the fact that it does not rust, makes it a common choice for jewelry. But gold isn't used for jewelry alone, although this may be why you're familiar with it. Chemists also complete chemical reactions with gold in order to make medicines used to treat arthritis.

Because gold does not react with other elements very easily, it is more likely to be found as gold chunks just waiting to be dug up. Most of the gold on Earth is found in the United States, Russia, Peru, Australia, and South Africa. As you may recall, all the elements are formed in stars. In gold's case, all the gold on Earth came here on meteorites.

 Discovery Zone Humans knew about gold before they were even writing stuff down. We have used it for so long partly because gold can be found in its elemental form and hammered into different shapes. For thousands of years, humans have dug it up or found it in rivers as the soil erodes away from flooding.

GOLD

MERCURY

Mercury is a shiny, liquid metal at room temperature. It has fascinated people for thousands of years. Unfortunately, it is toxic and can enter your body through your skin or when you breathe. It is also in our environment. Fortunately, our daily intake is less than 0.01 mg, which our bodies can handle. However, mercury can build up over time, so people are trying to reduce the amount of mercury in the environment.

It was once used in thermometers and batteries, but we are starting to find alternatives to mercury so we don't have as much exposure to it. Before the dangers of mercury were known, liquid mercury was even used to make felt hats. The people who made the hats for a living got very sick, which showed us the dangers of mercury. The Mad Hatter in *Alice's Adventures in Wonderland* is based on the fact that mercury often poisoned hatters, making them hallucinate. Mercury is still used for scientific instruments, but those instruments are used only by people trained in proper safety methods.

 Discovery Zone Mercury has been around for as long as we have had recorded history. A red mercury compound (HgS) was used in cave paintings 30,000 years ago. The ancient Chinese and Hindus used mercury as a medicine (bad idea!), while ancient Egyptians used it in their eye makeup. It has even been found in 3,500-year-old Egyptian tombs. The symbol Hg comes from the Greek word *hydrargyrum*, meaning "liquid silver."

ELEMENTAL STATS

P+ 80
E- 80
N 121

State: Liquid

Atomic Mass: 200.59 amu

Density: 13.53 g/cm³

Atomic Radius: 223 pm

Element Group: Transition Metals

MERCURY

ELEMENTAL STATS

P+ 81
E- 81
N 123

State: Solid

Atomic Mass:
204.4 amu

Density:
11.85 g/cm³

Atomic Radius:
196 pm

Element Group:
Boron Family

THALLIUM

Thallium is a heavy metal and chemically reacts like its periodic table neighbor, lead (#82). A heavy metal is one that has a high density, high atomic mass, or high atomic number. In thallium's case, it has all three! In fact, while many people think lead is the densest metal, thallium has a greater density. While lead weighs in at 11.4 g/mL, thallium has a density of 11.8 g/mL. Keep in mind that heavy metals like lead and thallium are quite dangerous to handle (even deadly) and have been featured as weapons in movies such as the James Bond movie *Spectre* and in novels such as Ngaio Marsh's *Final Curtain*.

Flame tests were used for many years to identify elements. If you put sodium chloride in a flame, the distinctive yellow of sodium (#11) would be observed. If you put calcium chloride into a flame, you would see an orange color from the calcium (#20). If you put thallium into a flame—though you should not—you would see a bright green flame. Thallium comes from the Greek word *thallos*, meaning "green twig."

 Discovery Zone William Crookes discovered thallium in England in 1861 as he studied the waste produced from making sulfuric acid. When he cleaned up the goop and placed it into a flame, he observed the bright green color. Crookes and French chemist Claude-Auguste Lamy were separately able to isolate and collect pure thallium in 1862.

THALLIUM

LEAD

Humans from South America to Greece have used lead for thousands of years. We've used it for pipes, cups, paints, and coins. From the 1920s through the 1990s, we added lead, in the form of tetraethyl lead, to gasoline to make our cars run better. A metal carbon chemical, tetraethyl lead was everywhere for a long time until scientists discovered that it was not good for humans. Sadly, lead is very poisonous.

Thankfully, we have now mostly removed lead from daily use. It is no longer in paint or gas, although it is still found in car batteries.

Discovery Zone
Because humans have used lead for thousands of years, we do not know who discovered it. But the discovery of graphite, originally thought to be lead, still causes confusion to this day. Because of the mistaken identity, many people still talk about "lead pencils." Yet there has never been lead in pencils!

ELEMENTAL STATS

P+ 82
E- 82
N 126

State: Solid

Atomic Mass: 207.2 amu

Density: 11.3 g/cm³

Atomic Radius: 202 pm

Element Group: Carbon Family

LEAD

BISMUTH

State: Solid

Atomic Mass:
208.98 amu

Density:
9.79 g/cm³

Atomic Radius:
207 pm

Element Group:
Pnictogens

You may be familiar with Pepto-Bismol, an over-the-counter medicine for upset stomachs that's pink in color and has a pasty taste. Its active ingredient is bismuth subsalicylate, a bismuth salt of salicylic acid. Bismuth subsalicylate works by coating your stomach, rather than being absorbed, to protect it from stomach acid and make you feel better.

Surprisingly, the pink color in Pepto-Bismol is not from the bismuth compound; bismuth oxide is used as a yellow paint pigment. Bismuth compounds are also in some skin products, creating milky white or "pearl-like" textures like those found in play slime.

Alloys of bismuth and tin (#50) or cadmium (#48) melt at low temperatures and are used in fuses and **solders**, metal pieces melted to create a link between two other metal pieces.

Discovery Zone Elemental bismuth can be found in nature, and the element has been known since ancient times. Because it is a silver-white metal, it was often confused for tin or lead (#82), which are near to it in the periodic table.

BISMUTH

POLONIUM

Polonium is found in very small amounts in uranium oxide deposits. It takes a lot of work to separate the polonium from the other elements, but once you have it, the nucleus of the metal will begin to break down, emitting small pieces of the nucleus called **alpha particles**. These alpha particles react with their surroundings and can cause damage, so the metal is toxic.

As the metal breaks down, it emits heat, which makes it useful for satellites and spacecraft. Polonium was used by the Soviet Union to power the first moon rovers, which explored the moon's surface. On Earth, polonium does not have many uses. However, a small amount of the metal is used in a special device used to remove the free electrons that cause static electricity. Static electricity is the crackling you hear when you rub a balloon on your head. Scientists use the antistatic devices while working with dry powders so the powders don't fly all over the lab bench.

 Discovery Zone   Marie Curie and her husband Pierre Curie obtained polonium from pitchblende, a mixture of uranium oxide, U_3O_8, and other radioactive materials. Several tons of pitchblende had to be used to get enough polonium to study. The Curies also found radium (#88) in the pitchblende mixture, and they were credited with the discovery of both elements.

ELEMENTAL STATS

P+ 84
E- 84
N 125

State: Solid

Atomic Mass: 209 amu

Density: 9.2 g/cm³

Atomic Radius: 197 pm

Element Group: Chalcogens

POLONIUM

ELEMENTAL STATS

P+ 85
E- 85
N 125

State: Gas

Atomic Mass:
210 amu

Density:
Unknown

Atomic Radius:
202 pm

Element Group:
Halogens

ASTATINE

The name comes from the Greek word *astatos*, meaning "unstable," so you can imagine that astatine is not a material you should play with. And because there is very little of it on Earth, you are very unlikely to ever see it. In fact, it has been deemed the rarest naturally occurring element on the planet. Most of the astatine that scientists have worked with was made in the lab by smashing bismuth (#83) with alpha particles.

The most stable form of astatine is still radioactive, with a half-life of a little over eight hours, meaning half of the material would fall apart in eight hours, changing into other elements. Astatine does not have any practical uses because it is so radioactive, short-lived, and dangerous to the human body.

 Discovery Zone In 1939, a couple of scientists were working on finding element #85 when they detected an element that was similar to iodine (#53) in a sample of radium (#88). Remember that all the elements in the halogen family have similar chemical reactivity. However, the scientists were not able to get the pure element. Dale Corson, Kenneth Ross MacKenzie, and Emilio Segrè created astatine in 1940 in the laboratory by smashing atoms with alpha particles.

RADON

If you live in a rocky area, you may have heard of a gas called radon. Mountainous areas have lots of **igneous rocks** that contain radioactive elements like radium (#88), thorium (#90), and uranium (#92). As these unstable elements break down, they release new elements, and one of these is radon, which can find its way into people's houses. Radon is harmful to breathe, but luckily, it is easy to remove from your home. You just have to use a special fan to clear the air from your basement.

If your house has a basement, you can easily test for radon using a testing kit available at most hardware stores. Each January is National Radon Action Month, which creates awareness about the dangers of this gas.

 Discovery Zone In 1899, Marie and Pierre Curie, along with Ernest Rutherford, observed a radioactive gas in their research of other radioactive materials. Friedrich Dorn was studying radium's breakdown and noticed the radioactive gas as well. William Ramsay and Robert Whytlaw-Gray finally collected enough radon gas to determine its properties. In 1908, the two scientists reported that radon was the heaviest gas in the periodic table.

ELEMENTAL STATS

P+ 86
E- 86
N 136

State: Gas

Atomic Mass:
222 amu

Density:
0.00907 g/cm^3

Atomic Radius:
220 pm

Element Group:
Noble Gases

RADON

ELEMENTAL STATS

P+ 87
E- 87
N 135

State: Solid

Atomic Mass:
223 amu

Density:
Unknown

Atomic Radius:
348 pm

Element Group:
Alkali Metals

FRANCIUM

Francium is another element that is very radioactive. You may have noticed that many elements at the bottom part of the periodic table are very reactive. It has a half-life of 22 minutes, so very little of the element exists on earth. An element with 87 protons was predicted to exist. Many scientists claimed that they had found element #87 but could not prove it.

Due to its super-short half-life, francium has no known applications. But because it's so rare, it would also be unbelievably expensive—if it were available for purchase. No one has ever observed even a whole gram of this element. If you don't know what a gram is: 1 teaspoon of sugar is 4.2 grams.

Discovery Zone In 1939, Marguerite Perey was working on radioactive actinium (#89) in France at the Curie Institute (below) when she discovered that a product of the breakdown was also radioactive. The new element had 87 protons and filled in a missing element in our periodic table. Because this discovery was so close to World War II and some people challenged it, Perey was not recognized for discovering francium until 1946.

RADIUM

Radium is an element found in ores of uranium (#92) and thorium (#90), though it has very limited use today. Because we are at the bottom of the periodic table, elements are unstable. The elements down here are larger, with bigger nuclei, so they tend to be radioactive and fall apart. This is the case with radium. You may have also noticed we have been talking about Marie and Pierre Curie, who discovered several of the radioactive elements and inspired more chemists to continue their work with them. It was the Curies who first tried to extract radium from uranium ore.

In the past, radium was used in clock faces and watches because it glowed in the dark. Unfortunately, factory workers, dubbed "the radium girls," began experiencing health problems, including cancer, from exposure to the element. Interestingly, an isotope of radium is also used to target cancer cells in bones. Radioactive elements cause cancer by damaging cells. So, it makes sense that we can also kill cancerous cells with very targeted use of radiation.

 Discovery Zone While studying radioactivity, Marie and Pierre Curie worked a lot with pitchblende, as you saw in our discussion of polonium (#84). In 1898, while studying pitchblende, they found that it was more radioactive than could be explained by just uranium. They worked very hard to pull out one milligram of radium (0.001 grams) from 10 tons of pitchblende. Talk about a needle in a haystack!

ELEMENTAL STATS

P+ 88
E- 88
N 138

State: Solid

Atomic Mass: 226 amu

Density: 5 g/cm³

Atomic Radius: 283 pm

Element Group: Alkaline Earth Metals

RADIUM

ACTINIUM

State: Solid

Atomic Mass:
227 amu

Density:
10 g/cm³

Atomic Radius:
247 pm

Element Group:
Actinides

Actinium is a rare element in uranium (#92) ore. It glows blue in the dark as it falls apart, exciting the molecules in the air. The blue glow helped give the element its name. The Greek word *aktis* means "beam of light." Because it is radioactive, it does not have any commercial uses and only has a few in laboratory research. However, it is sometimes used in radiation therapy for cancer patients.

Actinium is much easier to make than it is to find in nature. If you take radium (#88) and hit it with neutrons in a nuclear reactor, you can produce actinium. Actinium-227, a special isotope of actinium, is the most stable form of the element and has a half-life of 21.77 years. When actinium breaks down, it forms francium (#87).

Discovery Zone André-Louis Debierne, a friend of Marie and Pierre Curie (above), continued their work on pitchblende. He extracted small amounts of actinium from the uranium ore in 1899. In 1902, Friedrich Oskar Giesel independently found the element from pitchblende, not knowing that it had already been discovered.

THORIUM

Thorium is named for the thunder god, Thor, which makes sense because it's so strong! It's mixed with other metals like magnesium (#12) to make stronger alloys. Tungsten (#74) filaments are coated with thorium to extend the lifetime of electronic devices like televisions. One day, scientists hope we may be able to make electricity locally using small thorium reactors so we don't have to ship electricity from state to state over power lines, which can be wasteful (15 percent of energy is lost in transport).

Thorium, like uranium (#92), survives on Earth because it has isotopes with long half-lives, such as thorium-232, whose half-life is 14 billion years. Thorium is primarily obtained from the minerals thorite, thorianite (ThO_2), and monazite ([Ce, La, Th, Nd, Y]PO_4). Thorium, in the oxidized form thorium oxide (ThO_2), is used in **Welsbach mantles**, devices that produce bright white light when heated. This is how streetlights in the United States and Europe worked during the 19th century. Thorium oxide can also be used to make bowls used at very high temperatures, since it has a melting point around 3300°C.

Discovery Zone Jöns Jacob Berzelius (above) was a famous chemist known for the discovery of new elements in the early 1800s. So, it seemed like a good idea for Professor Morten Thrane Esmark, an expert in mineralogy, to send a sample of an unidentified mineral to Berzelius for analysis. Berzelius discovered thorium in Esmark's sample. Thorium was found to be radioactive by both Gerhard Schmidt and Marie Curie.

ELEMENTAL STATS

P+ 90
E- 90
N 142

State: Solid

Atomic Mass: 232.038 amu

Density: 11.7 g/cm³

Atomic Radius: 245 pm

Element Group: Actinides

ELEMENTAL STATS

P+ 91
E- 91
N 140

State: Solid

Atomic Mass:
231.04 amu

Density:
15.4 g/cm³

Atomic Radius:
243 pm

Element Group:
Actinides

PROTACTINIUM

Protactinium is not useful like its neighbors thorium (#90) and uranium (#92) because it is so rare and toxic to living organisms. The Great Britain Atomic Energy Authority was able to produce a small amount, but to get an aspirin-size sample, the agency had to process 55,000 kilograms of ore and spend $500,000.

Some people have tried to remove protactinium from used nuclear fuel rods and have successfully extracted a little. The most stable isotope of the element is protactinium-231 (protactinium with 91 protons and 140 neutrons in the nucleus), with a half-life of 32,760 years.

Discovery Zone An unstable isotope of protactinium with a half-life of about 1.17 minutes was discovered in 1913 in Germany by Kasimir Fajans and Otto Göhring. Otto Hahn and Lise Meitner isolated a more stable isotope, Pa-231, which has a half-life of 32,500 years, in 1918. Because there were not many uses for the element, there was no hurry to purify protactinium, but Aristid von Grosse finally did in 1934.

PROTACTINIUM

URANIUM

I n 1896, Antoine Henri Becquerel discovered that uranium breaks down as the atom's nucleus falls apart. This was the first time anyone had recognized that a sample was radioactive. Because uranium metal is reactive, it is usually found as an oxide (UO_2).

We use uranium compounds to generate electricity in nuclear reactors. The isotope of uranium needed for a nuclear reactor is uranium-235. This isotope breaks down when hit with a neutron to make two new elements and more neutrons, releasing a lot of energy in the process. We use the energy to heat water to make steam. The steam turns a turbine to produce the electricity we need in our homes. Unfortunately, naturally occurring uranium is made up of 99% uranium-238 and only 1% of the uranium-235 we need to make energy. Uranium is also used by the military for weapons and to power submarines.

Discovery Zone Martin Heinrich Klaproth found what he thought was uranium in pitchblende ore in 1789. He had actually found uranium dioxide (UO_2). In 1841, Eugène-Melchior Péligot finally isolated pure uranium by heating uranium dioxide with other metals.

ELEMENTAL STATS

P+ 92
E- 92
N 146

State: Solid

Atomic Mass: 238.03 amu

Density: 19.1 g/cm^3

Atomic Radius: 241 pm

Element Group: Actinides

URANIUM

93

Np

P+ 93
E- 93
N commonly 144

State: Solid

Atomic Mass:
237 amu

Density:
20.25 g/cm³

Atomic Radius:
239 pm

Element Group:
Actinides

NEPTUNIUM

Neptunium is the first transuranic element—the first element after uranium (#92). Because uranium was named after Uranus, the scientists decided to keep going and name the next element after the next planet, hence neptunium! Notice that you will see plutonium (#94) after neptunium, but you will not find jupiterium or saturnium on the periodic table. Different discoverers had different ideas about naming.

Neptunium is made during nuclear fission (nucleus splitting) in nuclear power plants. The neptunium is purified and used to make plutonium, which is then used for the power plants on many spacecraft.

Discovery Zone A lot of the transuranic elements were discovered in Berkeley, California. Neptunium was made in 1940 by Edwin McMillan and Philip Abelson. To make transuranic elements, scientists take a heavy element and smack it with another atom or atom parts. In this case, McMillan and Abelson hit uranium with a neutron, creating the new element!

94

Pu

P+ 94
E- 94
N 150

State: Solid

Atomic Mass:
244 amu

Density:
19.86 g/cm³

Atomic Radius:
243 pm

Element Group:
Actinides

PLUTONIUM

In the 1940s, during World War II, scientists were studying the radioactive elements to build the atomic bomb. These scientists had made neptunium (#93), and so of course it was natural to name the next element plutonium, after Pluto.

Plutonium was in fact used in a nuclear bomb. For this reason, a lot of people around the world try to keep track of all of the plutonium on Earth and what different countries are doing with the plutonium they have. Now that sounds like a tough job!

Discovery Zone Glenn T. Seaborg was the lead scientist on the team that created plutonium in 1941 in Berkeley, California. The discovery was kept secret until after the end of World War II to prevent the information from being used by the US's enemies. However, some scientists believe that in certain parts of the world, such as Gabon, Africa, enough uranium (#92) was pushed together that plutonium was produced naturally.

AMERICIUM

Americium, named after North and South America, is used in the smoke detectors in your home. Americium produces alpha particles as it breaks down. These particles consist of two protons and two neutrons and resemble the nucleus of helium-4. As they form, they ionize the molecules in air, which then hit the detector. If there is smoke in the room, the smoke blocks the particles, so no ions hit the detector, and the alarm goes off.

With a half-life of 432.2 years, the isotope of americium sticks around for a long time. Like other radioactive elements that make other elements as they break down, americium makes neptunium-237 as it decays.

 Discovery Zone In 1944, many scientists, including Glenn T. Seaborg, Ralph A. James, Leon O. Morgan, and Albert Ghiorso, were working in the University of Chicago's metallurgical laboratory crashing atoms together. They made americium by bombarding plutonium-239 with neutrons. Plutonium-240 was made first and then hit with more neutrons to make plutonium-241. The plutonium-241 decayed into the new element, americium-241.

ELEMENTAL STATS

P+ 95
E- 95
N 148

State: Solid

Atomic Mass:
243 amu

Density:
13.5 g/cm³

Atomic Radius:
245 pm

Element Group:
Actinides

AMERICIUM

ELEMENTAL STATS

P+ 96
E- 96
N commonly 151

State: Solid

Atomic Mass:
247 amu

Density:
13.5 g/mL

Atomic Radius:
245 pm

Element Group:
Actinides

CURIUM

Many of the radioactive elements have very short half-lives, while some stay around for hundreds of years. Some isotopes of curium can stay around for more than 18 years. It is most commonly used in the x-ray spectrometers of spacecraft. The spectrometers were used in landers such as the Mars rovers to study the rocks on Mars. Because of its toxicity, there are currently no uses of curium in our daily lives. Curium was the third element past uranium (#92) to be discovered.

Many people have heard of Marie Curie, one of the most famous scientists ever, partly because she was a woman working in science at a time when that was very unusual and partly because of her work in studying radioactive elements. Marie Curie and her husband, Pierre, made several discoveries, including the isolation of the elements polonium (#84) and radium (#88). While the discovery of curium was made by someone else, the Curies' work in this field led to the element being named after them.

 Discovery Zone Glenn Seaborg led teams of scientists to learn more about elements and radioactivity for decades, resulting in many element discoveries. In 1944, Seaborg's team discovered curium in Berkeley, California. Seaborg first revealed the discovery of curium on a radio show for children on November 11, 1945, and then it was announced to everyone else the following week.

CURIUM

BERKELIUM

97

Bk

P+ 97
E- 97
N 150

Berkelium is made by scientists in nuclear reactors. They take americium (#95) and hit it with alpha particles using a very large **particle accelerator** called a **cyclotron**. Particle accelerators use electromagnetism to get particles moving along a track at very high speeds. Hitting the americium with the very fast-moving particles produced berkelium-243, with a half-life of 1,380 years.

Unfortunately, berkelium does not yet have any commercial uses, and very little berkelium—less than one gram, or about the size of three small aspirin pills—is made in a year.

Discovery Zone Stanley G. Thompson; Glenn T. Seaborg; Kenneth Street, Jr.; and Albert Ghiorso produced the first berkelium in 1949. Alpha particles—the helium-like nucleus created by some radioactive elements—were crashed into americium-241 to create this new element, named after Berkeley, where it was discovered.

State: Solid
Atomic Mass:
247 amu
Density:
14.8 g/cm³
Atomic Radius:
244 pm
Element Group:
Actinides

CALIFORNIUM

98

Cf

P+ 98
E- 98
N 153

Californium, named for the US state of California, gives off neutrons as it decays. Remember, a neutron is neutral, meaning that it has no charge. A very small amount of californium (0.000001 grams, smaller than a piece of dust) emits 170 million neutrons per minute. The most stable isotope of this element is californium-251, with a half-life of 898 years.

This element is used for devices that find and analyze gold (#79) and silver (#47) ores. Another device, called a neutron moisture gauge, uses californium neutrons to find water and oil layers in the ground.

Discovery Zone Scientists Stanley G. Thompson; Glenn T. Seaborg; Kenneth Street, Jr.; and Albert Ghiorso produced californium in a laboratory in California in 1950. Helium (#2) **ions** were crashed into curium (#96) using a cyclotron. The collisions made short-lived atoms of californium-245, which has a half-life of just 44 minutes.

State: Solid
Atomic Mass:
251 amu
Density:
15.1 g/cm³
Atomic Radius:
245 pm
Element Group:
Actinides

ELEMENTAL STATS

P+ 99
E- 99
N 153

State: Solid

Atomic Mass:
252 amu

Density:
Unknown

Atomic Radius:
245 pm

Element Group:
Actinides

EINSTEINIUM

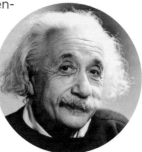

Einsteinium is named for the famous scientist Albert Einstein (right). Einstein did some amazing work that helped lay the foundations of quantum theory, needed to understand atoms and how they interact with each other. Einstein was also part of the first studies on **Brownian motion**, the motion of particles suspended in a liquid, which helped explain the existence of atoms. The element named after Einstein is radioactive; only small amounts of it are produced each year, and only for research.

Einsteinium's most stable isotope has a half-life of about 471.7 days. The discovery of einsteinium is interesting because it was found in the debris from a nuclear bomb test in the Pacific Ocean. Debris from the explosion was sent to California for testing. Two hundred atoms of the new element, einsteinium, were discovered.

Discovery Zone As we have seen, we make many of the heavier elements by fusing together the nuclei of lighter elements. So, we should not be surprised that a fusion nuclear bomb made the short-lived elements. The bomb debris not only gave us einsteinium, but also fermium (#100).

FERMIUM

100

Fm

Fermium falls apart through radioactive decay, so it is used only for scientific research. Its most stable isotope has a mass of 257 and a half-life of 100.5 days. Fermium breaks apart to form californium (#98) as it loses two protons and two neutrons.

The element is named in honor of the nuclear physicist Enrico Fermi, who helped build the first nuclear reactor. He was recognized for his great research with a Nobel Prize in Physics in 1938. His work led to the search for the elements that came after uranium (#92) in the periodic table.

P+ 100
E- 100
N 157

State: Solid
Atomic Mass: 257 amu
Density: Unknown
Atomic Radius: 245 pm
Element Group: Actinides

 Discovery Zone Sifting through radioactive nuclear bomb debris, Albert Ghiorso and his research team discovered fermium-255. The discoveries of einsteinium (#99) and fermium were not released for a few years because the United States and the Soviet Union were in competition and did not want to share information.

MENDELEVIUM

101

Md

Think back to the beginning of the book. Who developed the periodic table that we still use today? Dmitri Mendeleev! We think it is appropriate that one of the man-made elements is named for the designer of the table.

The first isotopes of mendelevium stayed around for only a short time, about 78 minutes. However, scientists learned how to make different isotopes, so they can make mendelevium that has a half-life of 51 days—a long time for an artificial element. But there is still no industrial use for mendelevium.

P+ 101
E- 101
N 157

State: Solid
Atomic Mass: 258 amu
Density: Unknown
Atomic Radius: 246 pm
Element Group: Actinides

 Discovery Zone A team of scientists in Berkeley, California first created mendelevium in 1955. Albert Ghiorso and his team used a cyclotron (see lawrencium, page 118) to combine einsteinium (#99) with helium (#2).

P+ 102
E- 102
N 157

State: Solid

Atomic Mass:
259 amu

Density:
Unknown

Atomic Radius:
246 pm

Element Group:
Actinides

NOBELIUM

There are no uses for nobelium, a radioactive metal. Only a few atoms have ever been made because it breaks down quickly. Its main use is to recognize a giant in science, Alfred Nobel. You may know of Nobel because of the Nobel Prizes. The Nobel Prizes in chemistry, physics, peace, medicine, and literature honor achievements "for the greatest benefit to humankind."

Ironically, part of the reason the awards were set up was that Nobel felt bad about the use of his invention—dynamite—and wanted to recognize people who use science for good.

 Discovery Zone A team led by Georgy Flyorov in Russia discovered nobelium in 1956 but never reported it. The next year, the Nobel Institute in Sweden reported the new element, naming it nobelium. Meanwhile in 1958, a US team led by Albert Ghiorso also reported the new element. All the claims led to years of arguments. The IUPAC eventually decided to keep the name *nobelium*.

P+ 103
E- 103
N 159

State: Solid

Atomic Mass:
262 amu

Density:
Unknown

Atomic Radius:
246 pm

Element Group:
Actinides

LAWRENCIUM

Lawrencium is named after Ernest O. Lawrence, the inventor of the cyclotron. A cyclotron is one of the most important tools used to make synthetic (human-made) elements. For his invention, Lawrence won the Nobel Prize in Physics in 1939, and many scientists used it to make many other artificial elements.

Scientists smashed boron (#5) with californium (#98) to make lawrencium. One isotope of the element can last 216 minutes. That may not seem like a long time to you, but it is a long time for a synthetic element after uranium (#92).

Discovery Zone Depending on who you ask, a team led by Albert Ghiorso at UC Berkeley first created element #103 in 1961, or a team led by Georgy Flyorov discovered it in 1965 in Dubna, Russia. The two labs argued over each other's data for years, but eventually the discovery went to the US team, who got to name it. Don't be too sad for the Russian team; their proposed name was used for element #105.

RUTHERFORDIUM

Because the elements in the periodic table are organized based on the number of protons and reactivity, understanding our common elements on Earth helps us predict what other elements might exist. Scientists initially looked in nature for the "missing" heavy elements but could not find them, so they decided to make them in the laboratory.

Rutherfordium, like all the elements after actinium (#89), is very unstable and produced in a laboratory. The properties of rutherfordium should be similar to actinide elements like hafnium (#72), but it is—poof!—gone in seconds, so scientists know little about it. The radioactive element is named after Ernest Rutherford (above), a scientist who provided evidence for our modern understanding of the atom.

 Discovery Zone A team led by Georgy Flyorov at the Russian Joint Institute for Nuclear Research at Dubna created rutherfordium in 1964, while an American group of scientists led by Albert Ghiorso created more in 1969 at the Lawrence Berkeley National Laboratory. The two groups argued over credit for discovering ruthfordium and dubnium (#105) for 37 years. Eventually the two groups were each allowed to name one of the elements. The American team named element #104 after physicist Ernest Ruthorford, while the Russians named their element after their research location.

ELEMENTAL STATS

P+ 104
E- 104
N 163

State: Solid

Atomic Mass: 261 amu

Density: Unknown

Atomic Radius: Unstable

Element Group: Transition Metals

DUBNIUM

State: Solid

Atomic Mass:
268 amu

Density:
Unknown

Atomic Radius:
Estimated

Element Group:
Transition Metals

Dubnium was produced in a laboratory by smashing other elements together at very high speeds. Scientists first bombarded atoms of americium (#95) with ions of neon (#10) to form just a few atoms of dubnium and a few neutrons. In what is now known as the Lawrence Berkeley National Laboratory, atoms of californium (#98) were crashed with ions of nitrogen (#7) to form some dubnium and four free neutrons.

Once dubnium is formed, it stays around for just 32 hours, so don't expect it to be in your new electronic gadgets. In fact, there are currently no known commercial uses of dubnium. It is not found in nature, so it has no biological uses.

Discovery Zone
Dubnium was discovered independently by Russian researchers at the Joint Institute for Nuclear Research (left) and by American researchers at what is now known as the Lawrence Berkeley National Laboratory. Each of the labs claimed the right to name the element, and the scientists argued for years. Finally, the International Union of Pure and Applied Chemistry (IUPAC) had to step in and settle the issue. IUPAC decided the Russians would get credit. They named the element after Dubna, Russia.

SEABORGIUM

Not many people get to have an element named after them. Even more rare is getting it named after you while you are still alive! Glenn T. Seaborg (right) had that honor, although the element was named 24 years after it was discovered. Seaborgium is one of the transuranic elements and cannot be found in nature.

Most transuranic elements only stay around for a really short time, but seaborgium has a *really* short half-life—2.4 minutes. What do you do with 10 atoms of seaborgium that will be around for only a couple of minutes? Apparently, not much (yet)!

 Discovery Zone Glenn T. Seaborg was part of the scientist team (led by Albert Ghiorso) that created seaborgium in 1974 in Berkeley, California. However, during the early to mid-1970s, a team in Dubna, Russia, was also actively trying to make new elements. The United States and Russia competed against each other in sports, space, science, and, of course, politics!

ELEMENTAL STATS

P+ 106
E- 106
N commonly 163

State: Solid

Atomic Mass:
266 amu

Density:
Unknown

Atomic Radius:
Unknown

Element Group:
Transition Metals

ELEMENTAL STATS

P+ 107
E- 107
N 163

State: Solid

Atomic Mass:
270 amu

Density:
Unknown

Atomic Radius:
Unstable

Element Group:
Transition
Metals

BOHRIUM

Bohrium was named for the great scientist Niels Bohr (right), who proposed the atomic model most people use today (see "Taking Apart the Atom," page 6). Bohr did some amazing chemistry, opening up the **quantum world**— the tiny world of atoms and the particles that make them up.

Bohrium is created in a laboratory by smashing atoms together to make heavier elements. Several different elements have been fused together to make bohrium. Sixteen isotopes have been made of bohrium, ranging in mass from 260 amu to 275 amu. The longest-lasting one stays around for about 90 minutes, while some last only milliseconds (1/1000 of a second). With such low stability, bohrium is useful only in the laboratory.

Discovery Zone Bohrium was created in two different laboratories, Russia's Joint Institute for Nuclear Research (JINR) and the Heavy Ion Research Laboratory in Darmstadt, Germany. While the JINR created several different isotopes of bohrium from 1975 to 1976, the Heavy Ion Research Laboratory created bohrium with a mass of 262 amu in 1981. Peter Armbruster and Gottfried Münzenberg directed the *schwerionenforschung* (Heavy Ion Research) team credited with discovering the element and got to name it after Niels Bohr.

HASSIUM

108

Hs

P+ 108
E- 108
N 161

State: Solid
Atomic Mass: 277 amu
Density: Unknown
Atomic Radius: Unstable
Element Group: Transition Metals

Scientists will be the only people to encounter hassium, since it does not exist in nature. Hassium was created in the laboratory by crashing iron (#26) with lead (#82). Lead has 82 protons and iron has 26 protons, so if you jam them together you get hassium, with 110 protons.

Unfortunately the element is not stable. The most stable isotope of hassium has a half-life of 22 seconds. Hassium is extremely radioactive, and only a few atoms of the element have ever been made.

 Discovery Zone Like bohrium (#107), hassium was created in Russia's Joint Institute for Nuclear Research and the Heavy Ion Research Laboratory in Darmstadt, Germany. Peter Armbruster and Gottfried Münzenberg directed the team who created the element and got to name it. Hassium is named after Hesse, the state where the laboratory is located.

MEITNERIUM

109

Mt

P+ 109
E- 109
N 169

State: Solid
Atomic Mass: 278 amu
Density: Unknown
Atomic Radius: Unknown
Element Group: Transition Metals

Meitnerium is made through the collision of bismuth (#83) and iron (#26) atoms. Its most stable isotope is meitnerium-278, which has a half-life of 4.5 seconds. Only a tiny amount of this radioactive metal has ever been made, and it has no known uses.

It was named after Lise Meitner, a German physicist. Because she was Jewish, she fled to Sweden before World War II. She was the first to understand and explain nuclear fission, the method used to make energy in nuclear power plants and the key to making the atomic bomb! Her colleague, Otto Hahn, was awarded the Nobel Prize in 1944 for their work, while Meitner was ignored. Would you prefer a Nobel Prize or having an element named after you?

 Discovery Zone Peter Armbruster and Gottfried Münzenberg discovered meitnerium in Germany in 1982. It wasn't easy! Over a week of hitting bismuth atoms with iron atoms made only a few atoms, but it convinced other scientists that they had found a new element.

ELEMENTAL STATS

P+ 110
E- 110
N 171

State: Solid

Atomic Mass:
281 amu

Density:
Unknown

Atomic Radius:
Unknown

Element Group:
Transition
Metals

DARMSTADTIUM

Darmstadtium is one of the newer elements on the periodic table. Now that we know the trends of the elements, scientists are working in the laboratory to make new ones. This element was synthesized in the laboratory; none of it exists in nature on our planet. It was made in the town of Darmstadt, Germany, which is how it got its name.

Scientists smashed nickel (#28) into lead (#82) to create this element. The material is radioactive and is not very stable, with a half-life of 11.1 minutes. The short half-life means that half of the material you just made will be gone in 12 seconds. In one minute, you would go from having 10 grams of material down to 0.3 grams. This makes it difficult to use commercially.

Discovery Zone Darmstadtium was created in the Heavy Ion Research Laboratory in Darmstadt, Germany, in 1994 using a **linear accelerator**—a device that speeds up electrons and aims them at a target—to shoot nickel ions at a piece of lead for one week, resulting in one atom of darmstadtium-269, which lasted less than one second. The more stable form listed on the periodic table has a mass of 281. Peter Armbruster and Gottfried Münzenberg directed the Heavy Ion Research team that created it.

ROENTGENIUM

Roentgenium is right below silver (#47) and gold (#79) on the periodic table, elements that are valued for their beauty. However, don't go looking for any roentgenium mines because it is a synthetic element. And don't expect to find any jewelry made of this element, either. The most stable roentgenium we know of has a half-life of only about 100 seconds. Imagine trying to make a ring and putting it on in less than 100 seconds just to have it fall apart!

Not a whole lot of chemistry has been studied on this element yet, so we can't tell you much about it, but maybe you can help us out in the future!

 Discovery Zone A team led by Sigurd Hofmann in Darmstadt, Germany (flag of Darmstadt, right), created roentgenium in 1994. The scientists created three nuclei of this new element by colliding bismuth (#83) and nickel (#28) nuclei together. The name *roentgenium* honors German physicist Wilhelm Röntgen. He discovered x-rays in 1895, famously taking the first x-ray of his wife's hand. Röntgen named his new discovery x-rays because he didn't know what they were, and x is commonly used in math for an unknown.

ELEMENTAL STATS

P+ 111
E- 111
N commonly 169

State: Solid

Atomic Mass: 272 amu

Density: Unknown

Atomic Radius: Unknown

Element Group: Transition Metals

112
Cn

P+ 112
E- 112
N 173

State: Solid

Atomic Mass:
285 amu

Density:
Unknown

Atomic Radius:
Unknown

Element Group:
Transition Metals

COPERNICIUM

Copernicium is a very interesting element to chemists because based on its location on the periodic table, it fits into the transition metal location. However, calculations have led some chemists to think copernicium would be a liquid that behaved like a noble gas. Unfortunately, it is difficult to study copernicium because only a few atoms have ever been made, and they last a very short time.

The element may not be very well known, but the person it is named after is very famous. Nicolaus Copernicus (above) is an important scientist from the 1500s. As an astronomer and mathematician, he developed the model of the solar system that placed the sun, and not the earth, at the center. At the time, it was a controversial idea, but it led to more scientific studies and the beginning of the Scientific Revolution, which has allowed us to better understand our world.

Discovery Zone The element is a new one, only discovered in 1996 by a German team led by Peter Armbruster and Gottfried Münzenberg working in Darmstadt, Germany. They made the element by smashing lead (#82) together with zinc (#30).

NIHONIUM

Nihonium is radioactive and artificially produced. As the most stable isotope of nihonium lasts only seconds, it does not have any uses in commercial products.

Scientists use nihonium in the research laboratory to explore how atoms are made and how they break down. Once nihonium is made, half of the material breaks down in about 20 seconds (half-life of 20 seconds). When it breaks down (losing two protons) it becomes roentgenium (#111). Element #113 was named using Japanese characters *ni* and *hon*, which mean "sun" and "origin." "Nihon" is one of the ways to say "Japan" in the country's language.

P+ 113
E- 113
N 173

State: Solid
Atomic Mass:
286 amu
Density:
Unknown
Atomic Radius:
Unknown
Element Group:
Boron Family

Discovery Zone Scientists in Japan at the RIKEN Institute, a lab for physical and chemical research, made the first nihonium atoms. The International Union of Pure and Applied Chemistry confirmed the discovery in 2015.

FLEROVIUM

114

Fl

Like all the elements since mendelevium (#101), flerovium was made by crashing two atoms together. For flerovium, plutonium (#94) was smashed together with calcium (#20).

The element is named for Georgy Flyorov, the Russian scientist who started the Laboratory of Nuclear Reactions at the Joint Institute for Nuclear Research (JINR). The JINR has been responsible for the discovery of seven elements. Sadly, flerovium atoms are not very stable; its isotopes only last a few seconds at most! And—you guessed it—since only a few atoms have been made, we don't have any uses for it. Like all of synthetic elements, it is highly radioactive.

P+ 114
E- 114
N 175

State: Solid
Atomic Mass:
289 amu
Density:
Unknown
Atomic Radius:
Unknown
Element Group:
Chalcogens

Discovery Zone A team led by Yuri Oganessian first created this new element in 1998, but they did not announce their discovery until 1999. Scientists at the Lawrence Livermore National Laboratory in the United States were also trying to make the new element, but the Russians won this race.

115
Mc

P+ 115
E- 115
N 174

State: Solid

Atomic Mass:
289 amu

Density:
Unknown

Atomic Radius:
Unknown

Element Group:
Pnictogens

MOSCOVIUM

Moscovium, an unstable radioactive element, was made in the laboratory to examine its properties. To make moscovium, the scientists crashed calcium (#20) into americium (#95) in a cyclotron. Their attempts made just four atoms of moscovium, which all fell apart in less than one second.

The most stable isotope produced so far has a half-life of 220 milliseconds (0.22 seconds or ⅕ of a second). There is not a whole lot you can do with an element in less than a second.

Discovery Zone The Joint Institute for Nuclear Research in Russia, along with the Lawrence Livermore National Laboratory in California and Oak Ridge National Laboratory in Tennessee, were credited for helping create moscovium in 2004.

116
Lv

P+ 116
E- 116
N 177

State: Solid

Atomic Mass:
293 amu

Density:
Unknown

Atomic Radius:
Unknown

Element Group:
Chalcogens

LIVERMORIUM

The American and Russian labs working on livermorium were successful in 2000 after many attempts to make element #116. The scientists made livermorium by crashing atoms of curium (#96) with ions of calcium (#20). The livermorium they made did not last long—its half-life was only 0.0006 seconds.

A more stable isotope, livermorium-293, lasts a little longer, with a half-life of 0.053 seconds. It decays into flerovium-289 by losing two neutrons and two protons. Do you think you could make something out of livermorium if you had less than a second before most of it was gone?

Discovery Zone We have heard about the two laboratories responsible for creating livermorium many times—the Joint Institute for Nuclear Research in Russia and the Lawrence Livermore National Laboratory in the United States. They make a great team!

TENNESSINE

State: Solid
Atomic Mass:
294 amu
Density:
Unknown
Atomic Radius:
Unknown
Element Group:
Halogens

Named for the state of Tennessee, tennessine is the most recently discovered element, but only the second heaviest. It is important partly because it is thought that this element may be located on the "Island of Stability." This "island" is really just the concept that some super-heavy elements with fast half-lives may have isotopes that will stick around for a while.

When tennessine fell apart (and it did so quickly), it made a new form of lawrencium (#103), which stuck around longer than any other previously made form of lawrencium. This gives scientists hope there are even longer-lived elements yet to be discovered.

 Discovery Zone Scientists from Dubna, Russia; California; and Tennessee worked together to make tennessine. One of the scientists involved, Dawn Shaughnessy, had been working on creating the element for many years.

OGANESSON

State: Solid
Atomic Mass:
294 amu
Density:
Unknown
Atomic Radius:
Unknown
Element Group:
Noble Gases

Oganesson is the last element on the periodic table as of the year 2020. Calcium-48 was collided with californium-249 to produce oganesson.

Oganesson is one of two elements named after living scientists. The other was seaborgium (#106), named after Glenn Seaborg. Both Seaborg and Yuri Oganessian led modern efforts to create new elements in the laboratory, making our periodic table ever bigger. And while we end the book here, don't be surprised to hear about new elements being made as scientists smash heavy elements together in the future.

 Discovery Zone Oganesson can only be made in specialized laboratories. It was recognized by the International Union of Pure and Applied Chemistry scientists in 2015, even though the first data was collected on it in 2005. It took 10 years of data collection for the scientific community to accept the new element. Remember, science is not always fast!

THE FUTURE OF ELEMENTS

Humans have discovered all the elements on Earth. The last naturally occurring element to be discovered was francium (#87) in 1939. Since then, we have worked hard to add new elements to Mendeleev's periodic table, but making them takes a lot of effort, energy, time, and money. Using particle accelerators, we collide nuclei with other nuclei or neutrons to get the smaller pieces to fuse (or merge together), hoping to make new, heavier elements.

Scientists have now completed the seventh row of the periodic table with oganesson (#118). And we are sure that scientists around the world are trying to make element #119 right now, partly because science is about exploring, and partly because many scientists believe that we can make new elements that will stay around for a longer time. In other words, they may be stable.

Chemists and physicists are currently searching for the "Island of Stability," but we don't know how far away we are from that island. Maybe you will help us discover new stable elements in the future!

Glossary

Alchemists: Early scientists who believed they could change one element into another element, but because they did not understand the elements, they could not make it happen

Allotropes: Different forms of an element; for example, elemental carbon exists as both graphite (like that in your pencil) and as diamond

Alloy: A material made by combining two or more metals to improve the chemical properties

Alpha particle: A piece of a large atomic nucleus that has broken off, consisting of two protons and two neutrons and equal to the nucleus of a helium atom

Anion: An element that has more electrons than protons

Assay: To test a material for purity

Atom: The smallest stable particle of matter, which contains protons, neutrons, and electrons

Atomic mass unit (amu): Used to compare the masses of different atoms; one amu is defined by scientists as $\frac{1}{12}$ the mass of a carbon atom that has six protons and six neutrons

Bond: An attractive force, holding two or more atoms together

Brownian motion: The random movement of particles as they are hit by other particles, comparable to a very busy bumper car ride

Capacitor: The energy storage part of electronic devices, which evens out the electronic signal when the flow of electrons varies from time to time

Cation: An element that has more protons than electrons

Combustion: A chemical reaction between a molecule and oxygen, which produces both heat and light

Compound: When two or more elements (including a metal and nonmetal) found as ions combine because their opposite charges attract; a positive ion (cation) is attracted to a negative ion (anion)

Covalent bond: When two elements are connected to each other by sharing electrons back and forth with each other

Cyclotron: A device invented by Ernest Lawrence to move ions very fast, allowing for the synthesis of synthetic elements

Density: The mass of material in a given space, which is usually recorded in grams

Electrochemistry: The use of electricity to cause chemical reactions (for example, we can add electrons to cations to form pure elements)

Electron: A very small, negatively charged particle that wanders around the nucleus of the atom

Electronegativity: The pull an element has on electrons. Fluorine pulls electrons toward it the most and is the most electronegative element. Francium is the least electronegative element.

Element: A specific type of atom with a known number of protons in the nucleus, which defines the identity of the element

Enzyme: A large organic (made up of mostly carbon and hydrogen) molecule that speeds up chemical reactions

Fusion: The combining of a nucleus of one element with another element (or parts of a nucleus, such as one proton or neutron)

Galvanization: Coating a material like steel with the element zinc to slow the decay of the material

Gas phase: One of the three common states of matter, in which the atoms or molecules are very far apart from each other

Hydrocarbon cracking: Breaking large carbon molecules into smaller pieces

Hydrogenation: Chemically adding hydrogen to a molecule

Igneous rock: A rock formed as lava or magma cools

Ionic bond: A strong attraction between a cation and an anion

Isotopes: Elements that have the same number of protons but different numbers of neutrons in the nucleus

Linear accelerator: A scientific instrument used to make particles like protons or electrons move very fast in a straight line

Mass: The amount of matter or material that makes up an object

Metal: Elements on the left side of the periodic table that are usually shiny, flexible, and conduct electricity well, and that often lose electrons during a chemical reaction

Molecule: A combination of two or more elements formed by the sharing of electrons, usually a combination of nonmetals

Neutron: One of the three major components of the atom, which has no charge but is as heavy as a proton

Nonmetal: The elements that are not metals, usually located on the right side of the periodic table, and that, unlike metals, are not shiny, do not conduct electricity, and melt or boil at low temperatures

Nuclear fission: The splitting of a nucleus into smaller parts

Nuclear fusion: The combining of the nuclei of two or more different atoms

Nucleus: The tiny center of the atom where the protons and neutrons are stored, which, if a whole atom were the size of a sports stadium, would be about the size of a pencil eraser

Particle: A small object that takes up a defined spot in space

Particle accelerator: A scientific instrument used to make particles like protons or electrons move very fast

Periodic table: A chart organizing all the known elements based on the number of protons and chemical behavior

Pharmaceutical: A chemical that is specifically used for medical purposes

Pigment: A chemical that gives an object color

Picometer (pm): A measurement of length, equal to 0.000000000001 meters

Polymer: A large molecule made from many repeating units, similar to a freight train with each car being the repeat unit

Propellant: A chemical that can be used to create lots of energy or gas to push an object

Proton: The positively charged material of the atom; the number of protons is also called the atomic number and defines the element

Quantum world: Areas of our universe that are smaller than the atom

Radioactive: When the nucleus of an element is unstable and breaks apart into pieces

Radius: In chemistry, a length measurement used to compare the size of atoms, equaling the distance from the center of the nucleus to the outer edge of electron location

Rare earth element: One of 17 possible elements, including the 15 lanthanides plus scandium and yttrium

Salt: Any ionic compound made up of a cation and an anion (for example, table salt is composed of sodium cations [Na^+] attracted to chloride [Cl^-] anions)

Semiconductor: A device that conducts electricity better than an insulator but not as well as a conductor, like a metal wire

Solder: A metal alloy with a low melting temperature used to fuse or connect metal pieces

Spectroscope: A device invented to use the many different types of light to explore the matter in our universe

Superconductor: A material that conducts electricity with no resistance

Wave: A disturbance that travels through space, with peaks and dips, like light and sound

Welsbach mantles: Named after their inventor, Carl Auer von Welsbach, materials that glow very brightly when heated, enabling streetlights to become possible

Resources

American Chemical Society, acs.org

Brock, William H. 1993. *The Norton History of Chemistry*. New York: W.W. Norton & Company.

Hakim, Joy. 2004. *The Story of Science*, Volumes I-III. Washington DC: Smithsonian Press.

Hargittai, Magdolna. 2015. *Women Scientists: Reflections, Challenges, and Breaking Boundaries*. New York: Oxford University Press.

Ignotofsky, Rachel. 2016. *Women in Science: 50 Fearless Pioneers Who Changed the World*. Berkeley: Ten Speed Press.

International Union of Pure and Applied Chemistry (IUPAC), iupac.org

Jefferson Lab, jlab.org

Royal Society of Chemistry, rsc.org

Scerri, Eric, ed. 2013. *30-Second Elements: The 50 Most Significant Elements, Each Explained in Half a Minute*. New York: Metro Press.

References

About Kids Health. 2020. "Iron: Guidelines to Improve Your Child's Intake." Last modified January 23, 2020. https://www.aboutkidshealth.ca/Article?contentid=1916&language=English.

Advameg, Inc. n.d. "Chemical Elements." ChemistryExplained. chemistryexplained.com/elements.

American Chemistry Council, Inc. n.d. "What is Chlorine? Chlorine Story." chlorine.americanchemistry.com/Chlorine/What-is-Chlorine/Chlorine-Story.

American Elements. n.d. "About Rutherfordium." Accessed November 3, 2019. americanelements.com/rutherfordium.html.

Castellani, Michael. 2006. "Carbon." Marshall University. science.marshall.edu/castella/chm448/elements2.pdf.

Chemicool. 2015. "Alphabetical Elements List." Last modified July 25, 2015. chemicool.com/elements.

Chen, Sophia. 2018. "How Dark Matter Physicists Score Deals on Liquid Xenon." *Wired.* January 11, 2018. wired.com/story/how-dark-matter-physicists-score-deals-on-liquid-xenon.

Chudler, Eric H. n.d. "Lights, Camera, Action Potential." Neuroscience for Kids. faculty.washington.edu/chudler/ap.html.

Compound Interest. 2019. "Tellurium." compoundchem.com/2019/07/29/iypt052-tellurium.

Currin, Grant. 2019. "The Secret Life of Gold." American Chemical Society. Last modified October 2019. acs.org/content/acs/en/education/resources/highschool/chemmatters/past-issues/2019-2020/october-2019/secrets-of-gold.html.

Foley, Sean. 2014. "Arsenic Poisoning." Toxipedia. healthandenvironment.org/docs/ToxipediaArsenicPoisoningPageArchive.pdf.

Global Advanced Metals. 2010. "Applications." globaladvancedmetals.com/tantalum/applications.aspx.

History.com Editors. 2018. "Bronze Age." History. Last modified September 30, 2019. history.com/topics/pre-history/bronze-age #section_1.

Institute of Physics. n.d. "Using Magnetic Permeability to Store Information." Last modified September 15, 2015. iop.org/news/15/sep/page _66245.html#gref.

Jewelry Notes. n.d. "The Mohs Scale of Hardness for Metals: Why It Is Important." jewelrynotes.com/the-mohs-scale-of-hardness-for-metals -why-it-is-important.

LanthanumK. n.d. "The Colors of Chemicals / Complexes." LanthanumK Chemistry. Last modified May 8, 2012. lanthanumkchemistry.over-blog .com/article-the-colors-of-chemicals-complexes-104821449.html.

JLab Science Education. n.d. "It's Elemental: The Periodic Table of Elements." education.jlab.org/itselemental.

Lenntech. 2020. "Periodic Table." lenntech.com/periodic/periodic -chart.htm.

Lewis, III, James L. 2018. "Overview of Sodium's Role in the Body." Merck Manual Consumer Version (website). Last modified September 2018. merckmanuals.com/home/hormonal-and- metabolic-disorders /electrolyte-balance/overview-of-sodium-s-role-in-the-body.

LibreTexts. 2019. "Saponification." Last modified September 23, 2019. chem.libretexts.org/Bookshelves/Organic_Chemistry/Supplemental _Modules_(Organic_Chemistry)/Esters/Reactivity_of_Esters /Saponification.

Minerals Education Coalition. n.d. "Periodic Table of the Elements: Lithium." mineralseducationcoalition.org/elements/lithium.

Monroe Engineering. 2019. "How Vulcanization Improves the Properties of Rubber." Last modified February 7, 2019. monroeengineering.com /blog/how-vulcanization-improves-the-properties-of-rubber.

Murcia, A., A. Blanco, J. Ballester, M. Fernandez, M.A. Suarez, and R. Iglesias. "Tantalum Implants in Reconstructive Hip Surgery." *Orthopaedic Proceedings,* Vol. 88-B, No. SUPP_I (2018). online .boneandjoint.org.uk/doi/abs/10.1302/0301-620X.88BSUPP_I.0880054c.

NobelPrize.org. 2020. "The Man Behind the Prize - Alfred Nobel." nobelprize.org/alfred-nobel.

North Carolina Department of Agriculture & Consumer Services. n.d. "A Homeowner's Guide to Fertilizer." ncagr.gov/cyber/kidswrld/plant/label.htm.

Nriagu, Jerome O. 2003. "Thallium." *Chemical & Engineering News.* pubs.acs.org/doi/pdf/10.1021/cen-v081n036.p153.

Royal Society of Chemistry. n.d. "Periodic Table." rsc.org/periodic-table.

Scandium International Mining Corporation. n.d. "Scandium FAQ." scandiummining.com/scandium/scandium-faq.

Sharp, Tim. n.d. "Periodic Table of Elements." LiveScience.com. Last modified August 29, 2017. livescience.com/25300-periodic-table.html.

Socratic Q&A. 2016. "Chemistry: What Oxidation State is Iron in Hemoglobin?" Last modified June 27, 2016. socratic.org/questions/what-oxidation-state-is-iron-in-hemoglobin.

Technological Solutions, Inc. n.d. "Elements for Kids: Potassium." Ducksters.com. ducksters.com/science/chemistry/potassium.php.

Whitwam, Ryan. 2018. "Idaho University Misplaces a Small Amount of Weapons-Grade Plutonium." ExtremeTech.com. May 17, 2018. extremetech.com/extreme/268879-idaho-university-misplaces-a-small-amount-of-weapons-grade-plutonium.

Winter, Mark. n.d. "The Periodic Table of the Elements." WebElements.com.

Yirka, Bob. 2011. "Army Pyrotechnic Experts Find Safer Alternative for Green Fireworks." Phys.org. Last modified April 11, 2011. phys.org/news/2011-04-army-pyrotechnic-experts-safer-alternative.html.

Index by Elemental Groups

General Index

W

X

Y

Z

About the Authors

ROSE A. CLARK is a professor of chemistry at Saint Francis University in Loretto, Pennsylvania. She has a BS in chemistry from UNC-Wilmington and a PhD in chemistry from North Carolina State University. After working in neurochemistry for her National Science Foundation postdoctoral studies at Pennsylvania State University, she started her career at Saint Francis University. She very much enjoys working with students in the classroom and in the research laboratory. Investigating proteins' interactions with surfaces and the electron transfer process between proteins and metals has kept her students busy for many years. Conducting research also means grant writing, and Dr. Clark has received funds from the National Science Foundation, Alden Trust, the Society for Analytical Chemists of Pittsburgh, and the Spectroscopy Society of Pittsburgh. She works with Ed Zovinka to do outreach through their Rural Outreach Chemistry for Kids (R.O.C.K.) program. Rose has been recognized for her excellence in undergraduate research with the Pittsburgh Regional Undergraduate Leadership Excellence Award and for her mentoring of future scientists with the Centennial Award for Excellence in Undergraduate Teaching from Iota Sigma Pi, a national honor society for women in chemistry.

EDWARD P. ZOVINKA is a professor of chemistry at Saint Francis University in Loretto, Pennsylvania. He earned a BS in chemistry from Roanoke College followed by a PhD in chemistry from the University of California, Davis. After postdoctoral research at North Carolina State University, he joined the chemistry department at Saint Francis University, where he has happily been since 1994. He enjoys exploring the world of chemistry by doing chemistry research with his undergraduate students. To help his students perform research, he has been the principal investigator (PI) or co-PI on several successful proposals, including to the National Science Foundation, the American Chemical Society, and the Spectroscopy Society of Pittsburgh. He is strongly committed to improving science education, and for more than 25 years, he has directed the Rural Outreach Chemistry for Kids (R.O.C.K.) program that annually reaches more than 5,000 K–12 students in the central and western Pennsylvania regions, through 230+ different events. Edward's awards include a Pennsylvania Professor of the Year designation by the Council for Advancement and Support of Education, the J. Kevin Scanlon Award for the Promotion of Science by SSP, and being honored by the Carnegie Science Center Awards for Excellence in the university/post-secondary educator category.

Acknowledgments

We would like to thank all our students (especially those at Saint Francis University) for inspiring us to share our love of chemistry with everyone. We would like to thank Saint Francis University for giving us a wonderful place to achieve our career goals. Saint Francis University and the Society for Analytical Chemists of Pittsburgh (The Pittsburgh Conference) have supported us in our science outreach. Of course, we thank our children, who have also been great in allowing us to do chemistry experiments with them at home.